BEECHCRAFT
STAGGERWING TO STARSHIP

An Illustrated History

Edward H. Phillips

FLYING BOOKS
1401 Kings Wood Road
Eagan, Minnesota 55122

For over half a century. the name Beechcraft has been recognized as the premier builder of high quality, high performance airplanes for business and private service.

In "BEECHCRAFT- STAGGERWING TO STARSHIP", every airplane Beech has commercially produced is presented along with a narrative on its particular highlights. Experimental and limited production designs are also included and represent some of the most interesting Beechcrafts to make it off the drawing board and into the blue.

No attempt has been made to document the entire service history of every Beech airplane since 1932; that task is clearly beyond the scope of this book. Instead, information of a general nature that is of interest to the aviation enthusiast and laymen alike has been selected for presentation.

To supplement photographs and enhance information for major models, three-view drawings are included throughout the book that depict dimensions, airfoil sections and other technical information of interest to the Beechcraft aficionado.

The reader will find each model, type or derivative described with technical information, performance and total number built for each model year. Where applicable, additional information is given that may be of interest to researchers, aviation writers, aero historians and aircraft modelers. The following Beechcraft airplanes are described in this book: Single-engine, piston-powered airplanes: Model 17 series, Model 19, Model 23, Model 24, Model 33, Model 35, Model 36, Model 45, Model 77.

Multi-engine, piston-powered airplanes: Model 18 series, Model 25/26, Model 28, Model 34, Model 50, Model 55, Model 56, Model 58, Model 60, Model 65, Model 70, Model 76, Model 80, Model 88, Model 95. Single/Multi-engine turbine-powered airplanes: Model T-34C and T- 34C-1, Model 90 series, Model 99, Model 100, Model 200, Model 300, Model 400, Model 1900, Model 2000. APPENDIX A: Complete listing of Beechcraft Approved Type Certificates including model, ATC number and date issued. APPENDIX B: Compilation of Beechcraft airplanes by model, model year, constructor number (serial number) and total airplanes produced in that model year. APPENDIX C: Footnotes that contain additional information of reader interest on specific Beechcraft airplanes.

The author wishes to thank Beech Aircraft Corporation and The Raytheon Company for their assistance in making historical, production and archival material available. Particular thanks and appreciation to Dora Thomas of Department 81 Vault and Mary Hall of the Engineering Library, who patiently endured many research visits by the author.

Other Beechcrafters are deserving of special thanks, too, including Gib Urick, Bob Umscheid and Don St. Peter, who provided information on Approved Type Certificates. Bob Magness, Jan Gustafson, Dick Mullen, Lyn Roberts, Cecil Bundy and Jim Lary gave valuable assistance with commercial and military constructor numbers and production sequences of many Beechcraft airplanes.

Eric Griffin and Lou Johansen of Beech's engineering flight test department provided information on first flight dates for various airplanes, including numerous experimental models. Phyllis McAbe, Jo Will and Annie Johnson provided supplemental photographic material and airplane specification data of a comprehensive nature. Thanks also to Lloyd Aldrich, long-time Beechcrafter whose expertise on the Model 18 series and the Model 34 Twin Quad were most helpful. Historians Joe Juptner and Larry Ball assisted with photographs of numerous rare Beechcraft airplanes.

Special and sincere thanks to Barbara Harding, Max Prickett, John Cook, Kenny Freeman and Jim Zluticky of the Beech photographic department, whose talents and hard work provided much of the pictorial record used in this publication. All photographs are courtesy Beech Aircraft Corporation (A Raytheon Company) unless credited otherwise.

Other Aviation Titles from Flying Books

Wings of Cessna, Model 120 to the Citation III
by Edward H. Phillips

Cessna, A Master's Expression
by Edward H. Phillips

Travel Air, Wings Over the Prairie
by Edward H. Phillips

Speed, the Biography of Charles Holman
by Noel Allard

The 91 Before Lindbergh
by Peter Allen

DH-88: The Story of DeHavilland's Racing Comets
by David Ogilvy

Aircraft Service Manual Reprints
Piper J-3 Cub
Aeronca 7AC Champ
Aeronca 11AC Chief
Taylorcraft BC-12D

DEDICATION

Walter H. Beech

Olive Ann Beech

Walter and Olive Ann Beech were a team, a talented couple that had but one goal: to manufacture the finest airplanes in the world. Their enthusiasm, drive and determination to succeed was founded on far more than just building flying machines; it was built upon the solid rock of quality, strengthened by integrity in business and piloted by the unshakeable belief that a satisfied customer was the company's most important asset.

These values were an integral part of the organization from its genesis in April, 1932, through economic depression, the horrors of global war and the blessings of peace. At the company's helm until his death in 1950, Walter Herschel Beech became one of America's most respected and honored aeronautical entrepreneurs and an aviation legend in his own time.

But Mr. Beech was only half the team. At his side was Olive Ann Beech, who shared equally in her husband's desire to establish an aircraft company on the Plains of her native Kansas. In addition to having acknowledged talent for financial matters, Mrs. Beech possessed the ability to apply her acumen to the essential, daily affairs of the airplane business.

Upon Walter Beech's death, Olive Ann Beech assumed the duties of company leadership and met challenge after challenge without fail. Like her husband, she wasn't afraid to push Beech Aircraft Corporation onward and upward, encouraging innovation and application of advanced technology to new airplanes that set the pace for competitors to follow.

Yet, leadership alone does not ensure a company's success. The unfailing efforts of Beech employees, from vice presidents to production line workers, have contributed their skills and abilities to make Beechcraft airplanes the best that money can buy.

"STAGGERWING TO STARSHIP" is respectfully dedicated to Walter H. Beech, Olive Ann Beech and every Beechcrafter since 1932. Together they founded a kingdom whose realm is not of the earth but of the sky.℞

Copyright © 1987 Flying Books, Publishers & Wholesalers, 1401 Kings Wood Road, Eagan, Minnesota 55122

Library of Congress Cataloging in Publication Data

Phillips, Edward H.

Beechcraft
Staggerwing to Starship

86-81230

ISBN 0-911139-06-0

Printed in the United States of America. First edition.

On November 4, 1932, pilot Pete Hill took the first Model 17R Beechcraft aloft, thundering into the chill Kansas air behind a 420 hp radial engine. Lifted into the blue on negative-stagger wings, Hill's uneventful flight marked the beginning for a classic airplane and a humble start for an enduring company.

Walter and Olive Ann Beech founded the Beech Aircraft Company in April, 1932, along with engineer Ted Wells and business associate K.K. Shaul. Aviation was hardly new to the foursome, since all had served together at the Wichita-based Travel Air Company during the late 1920s.

Walter Beech had served as president of Travel Air and a secretary named Olive Ann Mellor kept the office running smoothly. Ted Wells had worked at Travel Air as an engineer in 1928-1929. K.K. Shaul was comptroller of the firm. Sold to corporate giant Curtiss-Wright in August, 1929, Travel Air continued to flourish as one of America's premier airplane manufacturer's until the Great Depression clipped its wings in 1931.

During his tenure with company, Walter Beech learned the intricate and complex workings of the airplane business, became a nationally-known aviator and was recognized throughout the industry as a practical, erudite businessman.

Olive Ann Mellor had distinguished herself as Travel Air's office manager from 1925 to 1929. She possessed a keen understanding and appreciation for the financial workings of the company and learned much about airplanes, pilots, the Department of Commerce and the aviation industry's unique mannerisms. She married Walter Beech in 1930.

Despite Beech's high position at Curtiss-Wright, he was restless, a man who tolerated flying a desk in New York City while he yearned to build airplanes in Kansas.

In the spring of 1932, Walter and Olive Ann Beech decided to risk all they had to get back in the airplane business. Armed with courage, self-confidence, determination and some hard-earned cash, the couple and their associates returned to the Peerless Princess of the Prairie, as Wichita was sometimes called.

Although Beech preferred to locate the new firm in the abandoned Travel Air factory on East Central Avenue, it was not for sale and Beech couldn't afford to buy it. His long-time friend and fellow pioneer aviator Clyde V. Cessna provided room in his closed aircraft factory near the Municipal Airport on the city's east side. In an interesting twist of aviation fate, the infant Beech Aircraft Company started building biplanes in Clyde Cessna's monoplane factory.

Ted Wells and his small engineering staff (including, for a short period of time, Dwane L. Wallace) continued to refine and develop the Model 17R followed by the first retractable Beechcraft, the Model B17L. Wells and Beech had collaborated on the Model 17R's intitial design when the two men worked for the Curtiss-Wright corporation.

Sales were slow the first two years, but by 1934 the company's financial condition was slowly improving and the firm was able to lease the still-vacant Travel Air facilities in April to handle increasing production demands. To Walter and Olive Ann Beech, returning to the hallowed halls of the Travel Air factory was indeed like coming home, a home that eventually became world headquarters for the company. Beech purchased the entire factory complex from Curtiss-Wright in January, 1937 for $150,000.

Throughout 1934 and 1935, the Beechcraft Model 17 continued to evolve. The 225 hp Jacobs-powered B17L and Wright-powered Model 17R were joined by the 690 hp A17F; an airplane that could outrun the army's best pursuit ships of the day with its 250 mph speed.

But big, gas-gulping radial engines like the A17F's Wright Cyclone were expensive and in limited demand. It was the B17L and B17R that kept the production line going, followed in 1936 by the C17L with its 225 hp Jacobs engine, the C17B powered by a 285 hp Jacobs radial and the more powerful C17R with 420 hp Wright powerplant.

In 1937, the D17 series was introduced with three different models available: D17A-350 hp Wright; D17R-420 hp Wright; D17S-450 hp Pratt & Whitney Wasp Junior. These new biplanes were not just revamped C17 ships...they represented a new generation of the Beechcraft Model 17 biplane with improved ailerons, full-width lower wing flaps, redesigned empennage and higher gross weights.

Although biplanes reigned on the production line, in 1935 Beech had his engineers working on a new Beechcraft, the Model 18 monoplane equipped with two engines, featuring all-metal construction and a cabin that could hold six in comfort.

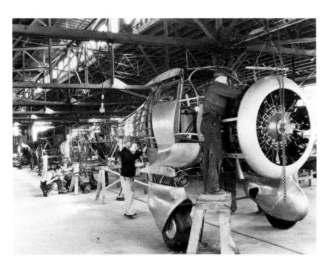

A17F c/n 5, NC12583, under construciton in Cessna Aircraft Company factory quarters leased by Walter Beech from 1932-1934. Note Cessna Model DC-6A and DC-6B fuselages stored overhead.

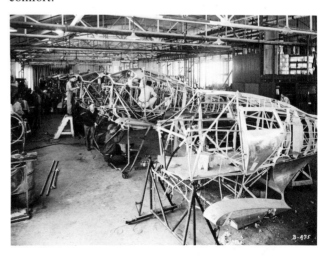

Model 17 biplanes were meticulously manufactured by hand. Each Staggerwing was essentially a custom-built airplane. (Jim Horne collection).

Designed for the businessman/charter airline market, the Model 18 quickly established itself as a popular load-hauler, particularly in Canada where charter and feeder airlines appreciated the airplane's ability to take wilderness abuse and operate on wheels, floats or skis.

Beech Aircraft Company reached a milestone in 1938 when it posted its first million-dollar sales year. The Model D17-series biplanes were continuing to sell and the Model 18 was finding increasing favor with customers around the world.

In 1939, the company's export business was accounting for a larger segment of its total sales than in previous years. Beechcraft biplanes and monoplanes were being flown in 23 countries around the globe...testimony to the quality and dependability built into every ship.

By 1940 the clouds of war had enveloped Europe and threatened to end America's isolationism. Walter and Olive Ann Beech knew that if the United States went to war, their company would be called upon to produce aircraft for the allied cause.

To handle the expected demand, Beech stretched the company's financial power to the limit and then secured money from the government's Reconstruction Finance Company to rapidly expand production facilities.

The engineering department worked hard and long to design airplanes tailor-made for training fledgling pilots, navigators and bombardiers. Their efforts at the drafting table resulted in the army AT-11 and navy SNB bombing and gunnery trainers, based largely on the civil, prewar Model C18S.

Further development led to the AT-7 and SNB-2 navigation trainers in addition to the C-45 military transport used for liason and general cargo duty.

To meet the increasing demand for multi-engine pilot trainers, Ted Wells and his engineers created the all-new, twin-engine AT-10. Built primarily of plywood to conserve aluminum, the AT-10 used metal only for the engine cowlings and cockpit section. Serving alongside the Cessna AT-17 'Bobcat', Beech's AT-10 helped train thousands of U.S. Army Air Force multi-engine pilots during World War Two.

Although monoplane Beechcrafts dominated wartime contracts, the rugged Model D17S was not overlooked for duty with Uncle Sam and his allies. Designated UC-43 for the army and GB-1/GB-2 for the navy, these rough-and-ready biplanes served in the European, Pacific and China-Burma-India Theaters of War as fast, comfortable personnel and light cargo transports.

In 1943, the Douglas Aircraft Company called upon Beech to produce wing/nacelle assemblies for its A-26 'Invader' medium bomber, being built in Tulsa, Oklahoma. Beechcrafters from the president on down responded and by

Beech Aircraft Company factory, located in ex-Travel Air buildings, on East Central Avenue, Wichita, Kansas in 1934, soon after Beech leased the facility from Curtiss-Wright and transferred production from Cessna factory.

1945, when production stopped, a total of 1,635 complete wing/nacelle sets had been delivered to Douglas.

During 1944, the Allies were gaining victory on every front, and on the homefront Beechcraft was continuing to do its part in ending the war. A quiet but critical part of that effort was performed by Beech engineers when they designed the Model 28 'Destroyer', designated XA-38 'Grizzly' by the U.S.A.F.

Bearing superficial resemblance to the tried and true Model 18, the XA-38 was, however, a completely new airplane and shared only the Model 18's twin tail arrangement. With a wingspan of 67 feet, length of over 51 feet and a gross weight of 29,900 pounds, the 'Grizzly' was powered by two Wright Cyclone radial engines developing over 2,000 hp each.

Intended to satisfy the Army Air Force's need for a ground attack airplane, the Model 28 was all-metal and armed with dual, twin .50-caliber remotely-controlled turrets and two .50-caliber machine guns in the nose section. But the XA-38's knock-out punch came from a 75 mm cannon located in the forward nose cowl.

Only two XA-38's were built and both performed admirably during exhaustive flight and armament testing, but the war was winding down and the need for such an advanced ground attack aircraft was no longer deemed necessary.

In 1945, victory in Europe was followed by victory over Japan and every Beechcrafter could lay down his wartime

Inflight view of first Model 18 with 320 hp Wright powerplants.

AT-11 formation over the desert Southwest on a training flight.

Profile view of powerful XA-38 Grizzly. Note wing hardpoint, entry ladder below center fuselage section.

tools. The company had produced approximately 7,400 complete airplanes and won the distinguished Army/Navy "E" award five times...a clear testimony to the company's ability to consistently produce the weapons of war.

Beech Aircraft Company had started with only 6 employees in April, 1932, grew to 220 by April, 1937 and increased to 780 by spring, 1940 when war threatened America's shores. In April, 1941 employment stood at 2,354, reached 10,950 two years later and peaked in February, 1945 at 14,110.

In making the transition from wartime to peacetime production, Beech engineers were ready with the Model D18S. Improvements included a 20% higher gross weight, redesigned landing gear, longer nacelles and a new instrument panel. The D18S held the distinction of being the first commercial, multi-engine airplane seating six to nine occupants to receive an Approved Type Certificate after the war.

The new Twin Beech sold well and production reached two per day as executives and businessmen lined up to take delivery of their office on wings. Another special Beechcraft introduced after the war was the Model 18C/CT specifically designed for small airline service or for heavy load carrying requirements. Powered with 525 hp (takeoff rating, 500 hp continuous) Continental engines, the D18C/CT was certified to stringent requirements of CAR (Civil Aviation Regulations) Part 04 for air carrier operations.

The future clearly lay with the all-metal, monoplane D18S,

but Walter Beech believed there was still a market for the aging yet superlative Model 17. Changes were made that created the final variant of this classic biplane, designated Model G17S.

A new, longer cowling surrounded the dependable Pratt & Whitney R-985 radial engine of 450 hp. An enlarged empennage and redesigned instrument panel completed the transformation.

The cost of manufacturing the G17S was simply too high. Most of the airplane was hand-made, especially the wood wings and fairing structures. Many of its parts and sub-assemblies did not lend themselves to mass production techniques.

Walter Beech knew the G17S was the best Staggerwing yet, but it would cost too much to build which meant it would cost too much to buy, and the production line never got started. Parts and assemblies for 20 airplanes were completed in 1946, but the airplanes were only assembled when purchased. Some customers supplied their own R-985 engine to save money, since the G17S was expected to cost approximately $29,000 with a new Wasp Jr.

A secondary reason for letting the G17S fade away was the new, all-metal Model 35 Bonanza, first flown in December, 1945. Powered with a 165 hp Continental engine and featuring a distinctive V-tail empennage design, the Bonanza carried four in a comfortable cabin, featured retractable tricycle gear, 180 mph speeds and cost only $7,975.

Initial deliveries of the Model 35 began in February, 1947. One Bonanza became the most famous Beechcraft to date when Captain William P. Odom flew his airplane, dubbed

August 2, 1948 photograph of Model 34 Twin Quad.

U.S. Air Force T-34A on acceptance flight over Kansas Plains.

the "Waikiki Beech" non-stop from Honolulu, Territory of Hawaii, to Teterboro Airport, New Jersey in March, 1949.

Odom covered 5,273 flight miles in 36 hours, two minutes and established a world record for Category III light airplanes. The 165 hp Continental engine consumed only 272.25 gallons of fuel and six quarts of oil. Total fuel cost amounted to a mere $75.

In 1947, Beech introduced the Model 34 "Twin Quad" feeder airliner that also utilized a V-tail. Designed to carry 20 passengers, the high-wing monoplane featured two engines coupled together driving a single propeller in each wing. While the Model 34 met all design goals and had good sales potential, the feeder airline market failed to materialize.

The Model 34 was damaged beyond repair on January 17, 1949 when a minor electrical fire occurred in the cockpit, not long after takeoff. All four engines were accidently shut down when the emergency master switch was inadvertently selected off. With little altitude to work with, the flight crew put the Twin-Quad down in rough terrain. It was an unfortunate end to a very innovative and promising design.

Beech introduced the Model 45 Mentor, a two-seat military trainer derivative of the Bonanza, in 1949. In 1950, the U.S. Air Force placed an order for the Beechcraft Mentor, designating it YT-34. After evaluation and service testing, the Air Force ordered T-34A Mentors and put them to work teaching cadet fledglings to fly.

The Mentor's popularity soon spread, with the U.S. Navy ordering the T-34B version in 1954 and the Chilean government placed a $1 million order for the export Model B45 in 1953. Other Central and South American countries who flew the Beech Mentor were Argentina, Colombia, El Salvador and Venezuela. Mexico, Spain and Turkey also flew the Model B45.

In 1953, Fuji Heavy Industries, Inc. of Tokyo was granted a license to build the Model 45, followed by the Canadian Car and Foundry Co., Ltd. that produced T-34s for the Royal Canadian Air Force. In 1956, Argentina became the third foreign country to build Mentors under an agreement with Beech Aircraft Corporation. The Argentine airplanes were assembled from units built at the Wichita factory.

As the decade of the 1950's arrived, the company was saddened by the death of Walter H. Beech on November 29, 1950. Olive Ann Beech succeeded her husband as president and chief executive officer of the company in December. In typical Beechcrafter spirit, business continued although Mr. Beech's presence was sorely missed.

The Model 50 Twin Bonanza and T-36A military twin-engine trainer were just two of the new Beechcrafts that were built in 1949 and 1951 respectively. The T-36A never flew because the Air Force contract was cancelled, but the Twin Bonanza became a popular aircraft with businessmen and pilots.

Beech did its part to fight Communist aggression in South Korea by building jettisonable fuel tanks and napalm tanks, complete wing sets for Lockheed T-33 jet trainers and ailerons for Boeing's B-47 "Stratojet" bomber.

Despite the war effort, commercial activity continued and 1953 saw the U.S. Navy order its own version of the Mentor, designated T-34B. Based at Corry Field in Pensacola, Florida, the navy flew the T-34B as its primary trainer until the late 1970s when advanced turboprop Beechcraft T-34Cs took over the training role.

As the 1950s progressed, Beech designed the Model 73 Jet Mentor in its bid for a USAF/U.S. Navy advanced trainer contract. Although the Model 73 flew well and was a low-

Experimental Model 35 Bonanza in flight. A classic design.

cost airplane based on the successful T-34 series, it did not receive a production order.

1955 saw the company capture exclusive North American marketing and production rights for the French-built Morane-Saulnier MS 760 "Paris" business jet and the Beech Missile Division captured a U.S. Navy contract for the KDB-1 target drone.

First flight of another new Beechcraft took place in August, 1956 when the Model 95 Travel Air light twin roared aloft. Marketed between the Model 35 Bonanza and Model 50 Twin Bonanza, the Travel Air was a favorite with pilots making the step up to multi-engine performance.

By 1958 the ubiquitous Model 18 had evolved into the Super 18 and was still selling well. Beech was also producing the F50 and D50 Twin Bonanzas. The J35 Bonanza received a fuel injected engine and the company reported increases in military and export sales.

In July, 1958 another Beechcraft Bonanza made history when Marion "Pat" Boling flew his J35 "Philippine Bonanza" from the Manila International Airport at Luzon, Philippines to Pendleton, Oregon in 45 hours, 43 minutes, breaking the existing non-stop record held by Bill Odom in 1949. Boling's triumphant flight once again echoed the well-known statement, "It takes a Beechcraft to beat a Beechcraft".

Beech sold the famous "Philippine Bonanza" to Peter Gluckmann in January, 1960. Gluckmann had made long distance flights in his own earlier-model Bonanza, but wanted to break Boling's record and modifed the airplane with additional fuel tanks and installed a 260 hp Continental (Beech sold the airplane without the engine).

Intending to fly non-stop from Hong Kong to the United

Prototype Model 50 Twin-Bonanza ready for maiden flight, November, 1949. Test pilot was Vern L. Carstens.

Flight view of Pat Boling's record-setting "Philippine Bonanza", N35U. Note wing tip tanks.

1960 Model G18S at the Beech factory. Note two-piece windshield, aerodynamic wing tips and taller tailwheel structure.

States, Gluckmann's first attempt failed due to severe weather. In April, 1960 he attempted a second crossing. Last radio contact with Gluckmann came 7 1/2 hours into the flight. He is presumed to have crashed into the vast Pacific Ocean somewhere between Japan and Midway Island.

The Model 18's long-time dominance was challenged in 1959 when the Model 65 Queen Air was introduced, setting new standards of Beechcraft speed, comfort and overall performance. It was also the first year for the Model 33 Debonair, designed as a less expensive, conventional empennage cousin to the V-tail Bonanza.

To augment its ever-expanding product line, Beech introduced the Model 55 Baron series in 1961. Carrying up to five occupants, the Baron had a maximum speed of 236 mph and paved the way for evolutionary versions like the Model 58, 58TC and 58P developed in the 1970s.

Beech entered a different segment of the light, single-engine market in 1963 with introduction of the Model 23 "Musketeer" and announced in August that the turboprop Model 90 King Air would be available in the 1964 model year.

Using Pratt & Whitney PT6-6 engines, the Model 90 heralded a new era in the Beech dynasty...the turbine era that would eventually make King Airs the world's most popular corporate turboprops.

The Beechcraft Model 60 Duke made its first flight in December, 1966 and fit between the Baron and the larger Queen Air models. Pressurized, fast and sleek, the Duke was Beech's latest addition to its high performance, piston-twin product line.

Frank E. Hedrick, Beech Executive Vice President since 1960, became the firm's third president in January, 1968

when he accepted the duties of that office from Mrs. Beech, who would continue as Chairman of the Board and Chief Executive Officer.

The Model 99, a 17-place commuter airliner, made its debut in 1968 as did the six-place Model 36 Bonanza. With a maximum speed of 204 mph and a range of nearly 1,000 statute miles, the new Bonanza featured double doors on the right side for ease of loading and unloading passengers or cargo. The Model 36 would prove to be the most versatile of all Bonanzas in the years ahead.

In 1969 the Model 100 King Air took to the sky as Beech's flagship turboprop airplane. But 1969 also saw the final chapter written in the history of the Beechcraft Model 18.

After building over 7,000 examples of the venerable Twin Beech, in at least 32 different configurations used in commercial and military service, production ceased in November. The last three airplanes, Super H18s, were delivered to Japan Air Lines ending 32 years of continous Model 18 production.

More than 14 years had elapsed since Beech Aircraft Corporation had become involved with the MS 760 Paris jet, but the valuable lessons learned from that experience led to the decision in December, 1969 to market the Hawker Siddeley DH 125 as the Beechcraft Hawker 125 corporate jet on the North American continent.

As the 1960s drew to a close, Beech had developed a line of airplanes from piston-powered, single-engine trainers to 10-place turboprop King Airs, and had the Beechcraft Hawker 125 at the very top of the list for those who wanted the ultimate in aerial transportation.

The six-place Model 58 Baron was introduced in the 1970 model year and featured the same double doors found on the

Model F90 prototype c/n LA-1 became engineering testbed c/n LE-0 in 1980. Garrett AiResearch TPE-331 engines were installed for testing as possible Model G90 that never evolved. Beech also tested more streamlined, raked windshield design on LE-0.

Illustration of Beech T-36A for USAF. Only one was built and never flew. Project was cancelled morning of test flight in 1955.

popular Model 36 Bonanza. The Baron 58 quickly became one of the best selling twin-engine airplanes in Beech's kingdom, owing to its generous useful load, high speed and ability to operate from rough, unimproved fields.

The company had also become deeply involved in the United States space program, beginning in 1954 when secret research began into the use of cryogenics as possible sources of breathing oxygen and electrical power aboard future U.S. space vehicles. In 1962, the company's Aerospace Division at Boulder, Colorado succeeded in designing a practical system for loading cryogenic materials aboard NASA's Gemini spacecraft.

The liquid oxygen was a critical link in the survival of the two astronauts since they depended on the Beechcraft system to supply both capsule pressurization and breathing oxygen.

The engineers and technicians at Boulder distinguished themselves again when they designed ground support equipment (GSE) for NASA's lunar excursion module (LEM) for the Apollo program.

Beech's Missile Division had also been busy through the decade of the sixties, developing the KD2B-1 target in 1961 for the U.S. Air Force and Navy that could reach Mach 2; twice the speed of sound while the Model 1025 target proved successful as a training drone for anti-aircraft missile crews.

With the dawning of the 1970s, Beech continued to develop the highly successful King Air series. The 1,000th turboprop produced was delivered in 1972, and that year was also the 25th anniversary of the Beechcraft Model 35 Bonanza. To celebrate the occasion, a specially-painted production V35B toured the country with the appropriate registration of N25AB.

Not one to become complacent with its dominance of the corporate turboprop market, Beech unleashed the Model 200 Super King Air in 1973 after four years of intensive research and development.

The Super King Air became Beech's new flagship, with 850 shaft horsepower UACL (United Aircraft of Canada, Ltd.) PT6A-41 engines, a graceful, T-tail empennage and increased cabin room and comfort for its passengers and crew. The most thoroughly tested Beechcraft up to that time, the Model 200 set a new standard for turboprop corporate airplanes and embarked on a course that promised to make

85% scale POC (Proof-of-concept) airplane used for in-depth flight and systems analysis of the Starship 1. POC was a flying testbed that enabled Beech engineers to develop and test aerodynamic concepts in actual flight instead of in a wind tunnel. Engines were UACL PT6A-135 rated at 750 shp. POC was built by Beech's subsidiary, Scaled Composites, Inc.

it as legendary as the Model 35 Bonanza.

The 1973 launching of NASA's Skylab orbiting observatory found Beech cryogenic systems on board, providing life support systems for the astronauts with the same reliability exhibited on the Gemini and Apollo flights.

In 1974, the company was selected to provide the power reactant storage assembly for the upcoming Space Shuttle Orbiter program, then gaining momentum. The system supplied liquid oxygen for the shuttle's life support system and liquid oxygen/liquid hydrogen to produce on-board electrical power. Drinking water was provided as a byproduct.

In the mid-1970s Beech engineers designed two new airplanes for the entry-level piston market; the Model 76 "Duchess" light twin and the Model 77 "Skipper" single-engine primary trainer. Both had T-tails and utilized bonded construction techniques in fabrication of the wings and tail.

The years between 1975 and 1980 saw introduction of the Model 58P Baron that brought presurization to the Baron line, making high altitude flights truly comfortable for its six occupants.

Beech also introduced, in 1976, the Model B100 King Air powered by Garrett AiResearch TPE-331 turboprop engines,

Beech engineers designed beyond Starship 1 to include a complete family of composite-technology airplanes. Cabin-class, twin-engine model illustrated is powered by two Teledyne Continental Voyager 550 engines developing 340 hp at 2700 rpm. Same airframe can mount two Williams International FJ-44 fanjet engines or two turboprop powerplants. Cruise speed (piston engines): 305 mph at 25,000 feet. All three versions are designed for pressurized flight and utilize the three surface aerodynamic concept: a forward wing, main wing and forward-swept T-tail. Piston-powered twin is illustrated.

Cabin-class twin-engine design mounting Williams FJ-44 engines.

marking the first time a King Air was not powered by Pratt & Whitney PT6-series powerplants.

A total of five King Airs were available to customers during the 1976 sales year: the C90, E90, A100, B100 and Model 200 Super King Air. Over 1,300 King Airs had been sold since 1964 and the company's 11-year concentration on the turboprop market had proven to be a sound decision.

1977 heralded another Beechcraft first: rollout of the 10,000th Model 35 Bonanza, signifying a remarkable accomplishment in American General Aviation history. A year later, the 1,000th Model A36 Bonanza was built and took off into the Kansas blue.

Continued success of the Model 200 Super King Air pushed Beechcraft sales higher than ever before, and in 1978 a Model 200 became the 2,000th King Air built. Introduction of the Model F90 King Air in 1979 added the sixth member to Beech's growing fleet of corporate turboprops.

With 750 shaft horsepower PT6A-135 engines, the F90 embodied all the improvements of the earlier 90 series and the T-tail empennage of the Super King Air. It was also the first King Air to feature the Beech-designed, advanced technology, multi-bus electrical system.

Beech had not produced a turbocharged Bonanza since the V35B-TC of 1970, but returned to the market in 1979 with introduction of the new A36TC. Boasting 300 hp from its Continental TSIO-520-UB engine (one of the first powerplants adhering to Beech's "minimum-engine" concept of rated horsepower plus five percent), the A36TC was a high flyer indeed, but Beech improved the breed in 1982 with the B36TC.

Featuring unique vortex generators on its extended-span wings that carried over 100 gallons of fuel (a Bonanza first), the B36TC's 300 hp engine made an altitude of 25,000 feet home territory for the best Beechcraft Bonanza yet.

After 48 years of ownership under the Beech name and decades of continued success, a major event occurred in the company's history on February 8, 1980. On that day Beech Aircraft Corporation became a wholly-owned subsidiary of The Raytheon Company, a Massachusetts-based, high-technology electronics firm with expertise in radar, weapons systems and commercial appliance products. Both companies found the merger beneficial, and at Beech business continued as usual, including production of yet another new Beechcraft.

To meet the need for a state-of-the-art, 17-seat commuter aircraft that would satisfy the growing demand of the commuter airline market, Beech engineers redesigned the Model B99 into the Model C99 Airliner in 1980, incorporating UACL PT6A-36 engines, improved hydraulic landing gear and featuring a gross weight of 11,300 pounds.

In January, 1981, Edward C. Burns became the fourth president of Beech Aircraft Corporation, succeeding Frank E. Hedrick who became vice chairman of the Board and chairman of the Executive Committee. Mrs. O.A. Beech remained as Beech's Chairman of the Board.

The year 1981 witnessed a significant honor for Olive Ann Beech. In July she was inducted into the Aviation Hall of Fame, joining Walter H. Beech who was inducted in July, 1977 at ceremonies held in Dayton, Ohio.

The Model 200 Super King Air received improvements in 1981 that resulted in the Model B200. PT6A-42 engines, higher pressurization differential, interior modifications and increased climb performance made the new Super King Air even more popular than its predecessor.

1982 marked the 50th anniversary of Beech Aircraft Corporation. The company had much to be proud of but spent little time celebrating its half century of success. There was work to be done, and one of the highest priority jobs was to design a new Beechcraft, one that would capture the attention of the aviation world just like the Model 17R of 1932.

In September, 1983, the company unveiled its answer to the next 50 years: Starship 1. Everything about the all-composite aircraft signified Beech's commitment to assert itself as the industry leader, a manufacturer that wasn't afraid to reach for the stars.

Starship 1 was designed and developed by a team of Beech engineers and Burt Rutan's Scale Composites company. An 85% scale airplane was built as a proof of concept (POC) testbed and first flew in 1983. Beech used the POC for testing the airplane's aerodynamics, basic powerplant and airframe systems installation that yielded information not obtainable from conventional wind tunnel tests.

Linden S. Blue became Beech's fifth president in 1982 and guided the company's programs until 1984 when James S. Walsh assumed the duties of president. Under Walsh's leadership, the company forged ahead with Starship development and revealed plans for a complete family of high technology, single and multi-engine Beechcrafts using composite structures and advanced aerodynamic features. In May, 1987, Max Bleck became president of Beech Aircraft Corporation, putting his years of aviation industry experience to work.

While Starship 1 certainly pointed the way toward the future, work continued on improving the highly successful King Air series, and in 1983 Beech introduced the Model 1900 Airliner, with 19 seats, 16,600-pound gross weight and UACL PT6A-65B engines. The cabin was pressurized and a rugged, high-pressure hydraulic landing gear system was standard. Many of the Model 1900's airframe parts and sub-assemblies were identical to the Model B200 Super King Air.

Developed simultaneously with the Model 1900, The Model 300 Super King Air was introduced in 1984, featuring PT6A-60A turboprop engines rated at 1050 shaft horsepower, multi-bus electrical system, hydraulic gear, four-blade propellers and a gross weight of 14,000 pounds.

The Model 300 quickly established itself as the King of King Airs and the company's turboprop flagship. It's high rate of climb up to altitudes of 35,000 feet coupled with high cruise speeds made the 300 competitive with small turbofan-powered corporate jets in terms of overall performance and price.

And getting into the jet market was exactly what Beech did in 1986 when it acquired the Mitsubishi Diamond-series, powered by Pratt & Whitney JT15D engines. A new interior, extended range fuel capacity and optional thrust reversers made the Model 400 "Beechjet" the company's premier performer.

Quality, performance and excellence in aircraft design have been the hallmarks of Beech Aircraft Corporation for over half a century. These virtues are an integral part of every Beechcraft ever built, from the bullish and beautiful Staggerwing to the sweptwing Starship 1.

The next 50 years will find Beech Aircraft Corporation ready to meet the challenges ahead, guided by the same spirit and courage that has made the name Beechcraft a legend in American aeronautics.

The Beechcraft Lineage

MODEL 17R - 1932

Designed by Ted Wells, five-seat Model 17R biplane had negative stagger wing layout giving pilot excellent visibility. Powered by 420 hp Wright R-975-E2 engine, maximum speed was over 200 mph. Faired, fixed main gear had electric motors that partially retracted wheels when airborne. Navy N-9 airfoil section was employed for low drag, high speeds. No flaps were installed. A unique feature was the electrically-operated pitch trim system that pivoted the entire empennage, not just the horizontal stabilizer. Color was overall insignia red with dark maroon scalloping. First flight: November 4, 1932. Pilot: "Pete" Hill. Licensed 499N, c/n 1. A second Model 17R, c/n 2, was delivered July 11, 1933. Licensed NC58Y and sold to Loffland Brothers Company of Tulsa, Oklahoma, the airplane was virtually identical to c/n 1. Pilot was E.F. "Eddie" Ross. Gross weight of c/n 1 and c/n 2 was 4,500 pounds. (Refer to Appendix C, #1)

Rare view of Model 17R, c/n 2 after being modified with full-swiveling tailwheel. Photograph taken at Cessna Aircraft Company factory site on Franklin Road (Pawnee Avenue). (Courtesy Robert J. Pickett).

MODEL 17R - 1934

Delivered to Ethyl Corporation April 19, 1934, original Model 17R was modified to suit its new owner with new paint scheme, narrow-chord, drag-type flaps under upper wing panels that were very similar to those installed on Model A17F; wider main gear and full-swiveling tailwheel of the A17F, c/n 5. NC499N was destroyed in a weather-related crash on December 10, 1935 at Nunda, New York, killing pilot Dewey Noyes. (Courtesy Robert J. Pickett) (Refer to Appendix C, #2)

MODEL A17F - A17FS - 1934

Powered by a 690 hp Wright R-1820-F11 radial, the Model A17F was built for the Goodall Worsted Company and Sanford Mills of Sanford, Maine. Delivered May 30, 1934, Robert S. Fogg flew the ship until November, 1934 when it was sold to Howard Hughes. It was entered unsuccessfully in the 1937 and 1938 Bendix cross-country races by pilot Bob Perlick. The airplane was destroyed by fire near Glendale, California, in the late 1930s. Capable of 225 mph, NC12583 was a high performance flying machine for 1934. First A17F was c/n 5, built during February -March, 1934. Narrow-chord flaps were installed on upper wing panels, ailerons on lower panels. Gross weight: 5,200 pounds. Beech also built one A17FS, c/n 11, in November, 1934, equipped with a Wright R-1820-F3 of 710 hp and gross weight of 6,000 pounds. Airplane was flown by the Bureau of Air Commerce from 1934-1937 when it was dismantled. Jack Wasall and future Cessna Aircraft Company president Dwane L. Wallace performed much of the engineering tasks for the A17F and A17FS along with Ted Wells. (Refer to Appendix C, #3)

Informal view of A17F c/n 5, NC12583, after factory rollout. Dewey and Blanche Noyes at left, Olive Ann and Walter Beech at right.

Profile view of powerful, bullish Beechcraft Model A17F, 1934.

MODEL B17 SERIES - 1934-1936

In 1934, Beech introduced the Model B17 series that were the first Beechcrafts produced in quantity. Offered with a choice of four powerplants, B17 series featured retractable landing gear, Clark CYH airfoil, ailerons and drag flaps on lower wings. Most popular was B17L shown here with Walter Beech. Powered by 225 hp Jacobs L-4 radial, B17L had maximum speed of 175 mph, cruised at 150 mph and cost $8,000. 48 were delivered from 1934-1936. B17B featured 285 hp Jacobs L-5, B17E used 285 hp Wright R-760-E1 and B17R mounted 420 hp Wright R-975-E2/E3. Because of the R-975's high price, the B17R cost $14,500. Only one B17B (c/n 20), four B17E and 16 B17R were delivered. One SB17L on Edo 38-3430 floats (c/n 40, NC15402) was built, in September, 1935. B17R was available on Edo 39-4000 floats. One B17R (c/n 72, NC15817) impressed by military as UC-43H during World War Two.

Factory-fresh B17L, c/n 15, 225 hp Jacobs L-4, August, 1934.

Hollywood actor Walter Pidgeon and actress Myrna Loy resting on the wing of an SB17L.

MODEL C17 SERIES - 1936-1937

The C17 series replaced B17 series in 1936. C17B was powered by 285 hp Jacobs L-5 engine and was the most popular C17. 40 were built in 1936-1937. The C17R featured 420 hp Wright R-975-E2/E3, had a maximum speed over 200 mph and a gross weight of 3,915 pounds. Beech C17R c/n 77 won the prestigious Bendix cross-country race in 1936, flown by Louise McPhetridge von Thaden and co-pilot/navigator Blance Noyes. They became the first women to win the previously all-male event. 16 C17R were

delivered. C17L was powered by 225 hp Jacobs L-4 radial, had a maximum speed of 175 mph, landed at 45 mph and cost $7,495 in 1936. Only six C17L were delivered. Airplane illustrated is C17L c/n 107, licensed ZK-AEU and exported to New Zealand for the Auckland Aero Club in November, 1936. C17E featured 285 hp Wright R-760 powerplant and two were built, both in 1937 and sold to Japan Airways Co., Ltd. SC17B (c/n 99, NC16440) was a Model 17 amphibian, built in 1936. One C17R (c/n 82, NC16434) impressed into military as C-43E . (Refer to Appendix C, #4)

14

First Model D17R, c/n 137, with ground-adjustable propeller.

MODEL C17R - (NAVY JB-1)

Walter Beech built good airplanes, and it wasn't long before the military establishment took notice of the Model 17's performance and dependability. In 1936, the U.S. Navy ordered one C17R powered by a 420 hp Wright R-975 radial and designated it JB-1. It was the first military Beechcraft in the sense that it was painted and outfitted according to the Navy's requirements. Assigned BuNo 0801, the airplane featured a unique, sweeping paint scheme. Beech c/n was 115, completed in December, 1936.

420 hp D17R in camouflage paint scheme, August, 1939.

MODEL D17 SERIES

In 1937, Beech introduced the Model D17 series incorporating major changes from the earlier B17/C17 airplanes. The fuselage was lengthened 13 5/16 inches, ailerons were relocated to the upper wings (flaps remained on lower wing panels), rib spacing was reduced to 6 1/2 inches, toe brakes were installed and a new, full cantilever empennage assembly was designed. Airfoil section changed to NACA 23012 series. Four versions were offered: D17A with 350 hp Wright R-760-E2, D17R powered by 420 hp Wright R-975-E3, D17S featuring 450 hp Pratt & Whitney R-985 and the D17W, a special racing model powered by a 600 hp supercharged, geared Pratt & Whitney R-985-SC-G radial (D17W did not receive Approved Type Certificate). 53 D17S, 10 D17A, 27 D17R and one D17W were delivered from 1937-1942. D17S cost $16,490 in July, 1937, had a gross weight of 4,250 pounds and cruising speed of 202 mph. Model D17R, NC17082 (c/n 137) is illustrated. SD17S version fitted with Edo WA-4665 floats. One was delivered in 1937. 25 D17S impressed into military as C-43B; 13 D17R impressed as C-43A; one D17A impressed as C-43F. The Model D17S became a hallmark airplane for Beech Aircraft Corporation. It set the standard for high-performance, single-engine private aircraft in the late 1930s, served with distinction in World War Two and remains one of the most classic airplanes ever built.

SD17S on floats. Note ventral fin and optional paint scheme. ▼

D17A, c/n 360, 350 hp Wright, for Brazilian Navy, November, 1939.

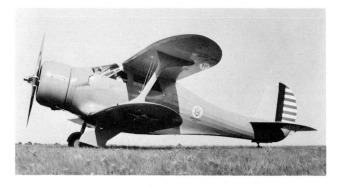

YC-43

Beech was awarded a U.S. Army contract in 1939 for three personnel transports, designated YC-43. Identical to the commercial D17S, the airplanes were assigned to air attache' duty in England, France and Italy. The three airplanes were: D17S c/n 295 (39-135) assigned to London, England; c/n 296 (39-140) assigned to Paris, France and c/n 297 (39-141) assigned to Rome, Italy. The first YC-43 is illustrated here, and was assigned to the U.S. Embassy in London. All three YC-43 were delivered in June, 1939.

MODEL 18R (SWEDEN) ➤

The Swedish Royal Air Force ordered one (c/n 321) Beechcraft Model 18R in late 1939 to be specially outfitted as an aerial ambulance. Designed to accept floats or skis, the airplane was delivered in January, 1940 to Kungl Flygfoervaltningen (SRAF) and shipped by sea to Sweden. Powered by Wright R-975 radial engines, the Model 18R was also ordered by the Republic of China in 1940. Designated AT18R, six airplanes (c/n 375 - c/n 380) were delivered, equipped with bomb racks, provision for fixed and flexible machine guns and room for a bombardier in the nose section.

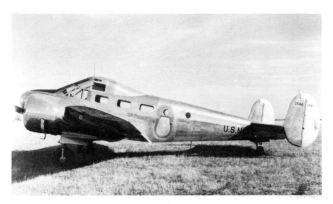

JRB-1

In 1940, the U.S. Navy ordered five JRB-1, outfitted with a special cupola above the cockpit for an observer who controlled aerial target drones. Beech modified the first Model 18S (c/n 222 licensed as NX19452 for experimental flight testing) with a sheet metal cupola structure. Five Navy airplanes were c/n 425 - c/n 429, BuNo 2543 -2547. All delivered in late 1940. Gross weight was 8,727 pounds. Powered by Pratt & Whitney R-985-AN-4 or -50 engines, the JRB-1 had a maximum speed of 225 mph. Beech also built over 300 JRB-3 and JRB-4 personnel transports for the U.S. Navy in 1944-1945 that were equivalent to Army C-45F transport.

First JRB-1 for U.S. Navy (c/n 425), October, 1941.

Wartime shortages forced the use of temporary wooden wheels on USAAF C-45A transports rolling off the assembly line. Sent to the "boneyard" for storage, standard wheels were added as they became available. (Jim Horne collection).

C/UC-45B

In 1940, the U.S. Army Air Corps ordered 11 Beechcraft Model 18S designated C-45 for use as general duty light transports. Painted with blue fuselage and chrome yellow wings, the first airplane was delivered in March, 1940 and the last airplane in August. Beech constructor numbers were c/n 364 - c/n 374, Army serial numbers 40-180 -40-190. After Pearl Harbor in December, 1941, Beech received contracts for thousands of airplanes and eventually built over 1,400 C/UC-45 for the U.S.A.A.F. All were based on the commercial C18S. UC-45B illustrated is Army s/n 43-35448, Beech c/n 5980. Engines were 450 hp Pratt & Whitney R-985-AN-1 or AN-3. Postwar derivatives of the C-45 series were: C-45G, TC-45G, C-45H, TC-45H, TC-45J, UC-45J, RC-45J. Great Britain received C-45 under Lend-Lease designated "Expeditor I" and "Expeditor II". The U.S. Air Force retired its last C-45s in November, 1963, after 20 years of service. Unofficial name for C-45 series was "Expeditor".

Instrument panel of UC-45B is typical of wartime C-45 series. Rudder pedals are equipped with toe brakes, autopilot in left side of panel has integral heading and attitude indicators. Throttles are in center of console, propeller controls at left, mixture controls at right.

C/UC-45F

Beech continued to produce the C/UC-45 series into 1945. C-45F illustrated was built late in the war and bears Beech c/n 7870 on fuselage and nose. Army s/n is 44-47462. Fuel capacity was 206 gallons, maximum speed 215 mph. C-45F could carry five passengers and two pilots in comfort, plus 80 pounds of baggage. Engines were 450 hp Pratt & Whitney R-985-AN-1 or AN-3. Army C-45F were equivalent to U.S. Navy JRB-3 - JRB-4 personnel transports.

SNB-1

Ordered by the U.S. Navy in 1941, the SNB-1 was designed to train gunner and bombardier personnel and was equivalent to the Army's AT-11. First production batch of 14 airplanes were built in August, 1942 and were part of the 73 total accepted by the Navy that year. 247 SNB-1 were built in 1943, when production was terminated. Machine gun turret was electrically operated. SNB-1 used turrets built by Beech and Crocker-Wheeler that mounted twin .30-caliber weapons. Bomb racks were built into the lower fuselage aft of the front spar and accomodated up to ten 100-pound bombs. 320 SNB-1 were accepted for service by the Navy during World War Two. Aircraft illustrated is c/n 4441, built in 1943. Beech adopted a thousand-series constructor number system in 1941 that was used throughout the war. SNB-1 was powered by 450 hp Pratt & Whitney R-985-AN1. Gross weight was 9,300 pounds.

SNB-2

Beech started producing the SNB-2 version in July, 1942, when 4 were built. The SNB-2 was utilized primarily as a navigation trainer and general purpose transport. Aircraft illustrated served the Air Force, Atlantic Fleet on the east coast of the United States. Photograph was taken at Norfolk Naval Air Station, Norfolk, Virginia. Navy PB4Y-1 in background was probably assigned to anti-submarine duty along the coast. SNB-2 was powered by Pratt & Whitney R-985-25 engines of 450 hp. Maximum speed: 225 mph; gross weight: 8,700 pounds. The U.S. Navy took delivery of 606 SNB-2 during the war. Deliveries began in 1942 with 44 airplanes, peaked at 286 in 1943. 276 were delivered in 1944.

SNB-4/SNB-5/SNB-5P

The U.S. Navy returned 117 SNB-1 personnel transports to the Beech factory in 1947 for rebuilding and modification that completely refurbished the war-weary fleet. Each airplane was disassembled, inspected and reassembled with new parts and assemblies as required. When completed the airplanes were re-designated SNB-4 by the Navy and continued their role as navigation and general transport aircraft. In 1951, a refurbishing program began at Beech's Herington, Kansas facility for U.S. Navy SNB-series airplanes. New, stronger wing center section truss assemblies and disc-type wheel brakes were installed. Hamilton-Standard "Hydromatic" constant-speed, full-feathering propellers were mounted and the engine nacelles were lengthened and streamlined aft above the wing. Major changes to the cockpit included new instrumentation for both pilot and co-pilot and installation of Sperry autopilots. The many changes and improvements brought the airplanes up to commercial D18S configuration. Designated SNB-5P by the U.S. Navy, a total of 2,263 airplanes were modified by Beech during the 10-year program. SNB-5P illustrated is fresh from Beech's Herington modification center.

C-45G/C-45H

The U.S. Air Force returned many war-weary C-45, AT-7 and AT-11 airplanes to Beech for complete overhaul and modification to the same Model D18S standards as the U.S. Navy SNB-5P, including heavier wing center section truss structure, new landing gear struts, wheels and brakes, instrument panel and avionics/instrumentation. USAF aircraft seated six and featured Hamilton Standard two-blade, constant-speed, full-feathering propellers as part of the refitting program. Majority of work was accomplished at the Herington, Kansas facility from 1951 to 1961. USAF C-45H illustrated is ready for delivery. Beech's rebuilding program for the U.S. Navy and Air Force gave military Model 18s a second life and many soldiered on until the early 1960s before being replaced by more modern aircraft.

AT-7

Beech designed the AT-7 to meet a U.S. Army Air Force requirement for a navigation trainer. Equipment included drift meters, work tables and compasses in the cabin. An auxiliary instrument panel with essential flight/navigation instrumentation was mounted in the front of the cabin for student reference. Celestial navigation sightings were made through a small turret in cabin roof. Thousands of navigators graduated from the AT-7 to B-17s and B-24s. 187 AT-7 were delivered in 1941; peak production occurred in 1943 when 361 airplanes went to war. A total of 884 AT-7 were accepted by the Army during World War Two. Powered by 450 hp Pratt & Whitney R-985-25 engines, AT-7 had a maximum speed of 225 mph, cruised at 190 mph. Gross weight: 8,727 pounds. AT-7 illustrated was completed in September, 1943. AT-7 was also designated T-7-BH. Beech records indicate 19 AT-7 were built as UC-45 series in 1943 for use as Army personnel transports. Unofficial name for AT-7 was "Navigator".

With gear retracted and cowl flaps closed, a Beechcraft for the U.S. Army Air Force rips through the Kansas skies on a test flight in January, 1942. (Jim Horne collection).

April, 1944 photograph of U.S.A.A.F. AT-7 navigation trainer.

AT-7A - AT-7B - AT-7C

The versatile AT-7 was designated AT-7A when modified to accept floats and skis. One airplane was modified with float and ski fittings in August, 1943, 12 in September and 30 more were built in October with the same modifications. Two 450 hp Pratt & Whitney R-985-AN1 engines gave the AT-7A a maximum speed of 210 mph, cruise of 174 mph. AT-7A illustrated on beaching gear with entry door open and special boarding ladder deployed. Large ventral fin under aft fuselage provided additional vertical area for directional stability with floats installed. Airplane is c/n 1176, Army s/n 41-21161 used to test float installation. Photograph taken on November 23, 1942. AT-7B variant featured special cold-climate equipment for possible sub-zero temperature operations and 450 hp R-985-25 engines. AT-7C had a more complex and sophisticated avionics/autopilot than AT-7/AT-7A/AT-7B, was fitted with 450 hp R-985-AN-3 engines. AT-7C also designated T-7C-BH by the Army. ▼

AT-7 trainer photographed January 2, 1942. Note rudder stripes. This airplane became the testbed for AT-7A float version. Turret above fuselage was used for training students in principles of celestial navigation.

AT-11 - AT-11A

Beech's AT-11 taught thousands of young men to say "Bomb's away!", dropping lethal high explosives on America's adversaries with devastating accuracy. AT-11s were based primarily in the southwestern United States where favorable flying weather prevailed and made almost round-the-clock training possible. Equipped with bombsights and racks holding up to ten 100-pound practice bombs, the AT-11 normally carried three students and a crew of two on training missions. A clear plexiglass nose dome housed the famed Norden bombsight. Some AT-11 were converted to navigation trainers similar to AT-7 series, but most were dedicated to bombardier training. Deliveries began in December, 1941 and 1,560 were delivered to the U.S. Army Air Force during the war. Peak production reached 749 airplanes in 1942. Beech delivered the last production AT-11 in May, 1944. Model AT-11 also designated T-11-BH. AT-11A was basic AT-11 modified for aerial photography missions. Beech built 42 F-2B versions that were equivalent to AT-11A. AT-11/AT-11A powered by 450 hp Pratt & Whitney R-985-AN1 or -AN3. Maximum speed: 215 mph. Gross weight: 9,300 pounds. AT-11 illustrated was completed in August, 1941 and displays its unique "bomber nose" section where student bombardiers learned their deadly trade. Aircraft is U.S.A.A.C. serial number 41-9437. Many AT-11s were converted to C-45G/C-45H configuration between 1951-1961. Unofficial name of AT-11 was "Kansan".

Profile view of U.S. Army Air Corps AT-11 bombardier trainer, built in August, 1941. Note red/white/blue rudder stripes that quickly disappeared after America's entry into World War Two.

Oblique view of AT-7A on floats with beaching gear.

"Acres of Beechcraft". Final assembly seemingly stretches to infinity. Believed to be a composite photo. U.S. Army AT-11 and Navy SNB-1 production line in December, 1941. Note pre-war red-white-blue rudder stripes. (Jim Horne collection). ▼

Model D18S owned by Hollywood's 20th Century Fox, August, 1946.

Cockpit view of Model D18S instrument panel.

MODEL C18S/D18S

In late 1944, Beech produced a small number of commercial Model C18S airplanes that were equivalent to the Army C-45F and Navy JRB-4 personnel transports. Originally designed in 1940, the C18S had minor structural changes from the Model B18S. Beech records indicate one C18S (c/n 432) was delivered to the Philippine Army Air Corps in November, 1940. C18S was the basic airframe used to build U.S.A.A.F. UC-45 -AT-7 -AT-11 series and Navy SNB -JRB series in World War Two. Engines were Pratt & Whitney R-985, 450 hp. When hostilities ended in August, 1945, Beech introduced the postwar Model D18S, very similar to the C18S but featuring longer, more streamlined engine nacelles and a stronger wing center section structure that permitted a gross weight of 8,500 pounds or 8,750 if Hamilton Standard Hydromatic propellers were installed (later modifications allowed a gross weight of 9,000 pounds). The cabin accomodated six to nine people in comfort. 296 D18S were produced in 1946...the highest number for any Model 18 in a single year. Beech introduced a new constructor number system after the war that assigned separate c/n for each model Beechcraft. D18S were designated by the letter "A" followed by the c/n. Records indicate that over 1,000 D18S were produced from 1945-1955. Powered by Pratt & Whitney R-985-series engines, the D18S had a maximum speed of 230 mph at 5,000 feet and cost $61,500 for the basic airplane. In 1951, Beech started production on the first of 283 "Canadian Expeditor" D18S for the Royal Canadian Air Force (RCAF). Designated Mk. 3N, Mk. 3NM and Mk. 3TM (desginated later as Mk. 3T, Mk.3TM, Mk. 3NMT) the airplanes were employed as communications and navigation trainers. Performance was basically identical to commercial D18S. D18S illustrated was owned by Hollywood's Twentieth Century Fox Studios.

Factory-fresh Model D18S ready for delivery.

Time Magazine purchased this specially-equipped Model C18S in October, 1945 for photographic and transport work. Airplane is fitted with door-mounted access panel for oblique photography that is identical to panels used on F-2 and other Beech military Model 18 derivatives. A lavatory was installed in the aft cabin.

MODEL D18C/CT

One of the most rare of all Twin Beech versions, development of the 1946 Model 18CT was inspired by the promising postwar feeder airline market. Designed to seat 8-9 passengers, primary change from the Model D18S was three-fold: two Continental R-9A, nine-cylinder radial engines rated at 525 hp for takeoff and 500 hp at 2300 rpm for climb and cruise were installed on the 18C and 18CT; the D18CT was designed specifically as a small airliner and featured extra safety equipment as required with the interior outfitted accordingly; the 18CT was certified under the stringent rules of Civil Aeronautics Authority Section 04 requiring additional structural integrity and rigorous testing before certification while the 18C was intended for executive service with custom-designed interiors and certified under CAR Section 03. Standard maximum gross weight was 9,000 pounds but optional gross weight of 9,450 pounds was permitted if Hamilton Standard Hydromatic, full-

feathering propellers were installed. R-9A engine was a new development in 1946, and Beech contracted to receive some of the earliest examples for use on the D18C/CT. Cruising speed was 224 mph (75% power setting) at 8,500 feet and maximum speed was 240 mph at 3,900 feet. Standard fuel capacity: 206 gallons with 47-gallon auxiliary tank optional (253 gallons total); range was 900 statute miles with 253 gallons of fuel. The D18C cost $64,250 and the D18CT (airliner configuration) cost $64,887 fly away factory (FAF). According to Beech production records, only 29 D18C/CT were built and delivered, but FAA records show 31 airplanes produced, starting with c/n AA-1 and ending with c/n AA-31. Of these, 16 were built as D18CT for feeder airline service. First deliveries occurred in April, 1946. ATC 765 granted D18C on 7-16-47; ATC 770 granted D18CT on 6-3-47. Model D18CT in the livery of Inland Airways is illustrated. (Courtesy Joseph P. Juptner)

MODEL SUPER E18S　▶

Introduced in the fall of 1954, the Model E18S was the first of Beech's Super 18 series and incorporated many changes. The most salient were: cabin height raised six inches for increased head room, four cabin windows, larger airstair-type cabin door, gross weight of 9,300 pounds, wingspan increased four feet to 49 feet eight inches (increase of 12 square feet of area to 361 square feet), new wing tips that provided increased single-engine climb rate and service ceiling. Pratt & Whitney R-985-series radial engines of 450 hp were installed. E18S was produced from August, 1954 until January, 1960 when it was replaced by the Model G18S. Records indicate 451 Model E18S were delivered from 1954 to 1960. Cruising speed for the E18S was 215 mph at 10,000 feet. E18S illustrated has landing lights in nose cap, custom paint scheme. Model E18S-9700 had three-blade Hartzell propellers and a gross weight of 9,700 pounds. Model E18S c/n have a "BA" prefix.

Model E18S instrument panel displays throttle, mixture and propeller levers featuring shaped knobs for easy identification, landing gear and flap controls located in center pedestal.

MODEL SUPER G18S

Beechcraft's Model 18 was 22 years old in 1959, but it continued to be in demand as a business and executive airplane largely because of its solid performance, dependability and investment value. Customer deliveries of the improved Model G18S began in December, 1959. The only major changes were an increase in gross weight to 9,700 pounds, three-blade Hartzell propellers and a new, two-piece windshield that improved the airplane's appearance and diffusion of rain. Minor change was a large, center cabin window that increased passenger viewing area. A total of 154 G18S were delivered from 1959-1963. 1961 G18S is illustrated.

MODEL SUPER H18

1962 marked the 25th year of continuous Model 18 production. In August, Beech introduced the Model Super H18, the last version of a truly great airplane. Gross weight was 9,900 pounds, useful load reached an all-time high of more than 4,200 pounds and maximum speed was 236 mph. The landing gear struts featured half-fork design instead of the full-fork used on previous models and smaller 8.50 x 10 wheels/tires were installed. Electric cowl flaps were standard and air conditioning was available for the first time in a Model 18. Lightweight, three-blade propellers were standard and the main fuel tank capacity was increased to 99 gallons. In 1963, Beech offered a choice of landing gear configurations; customers could order the standard, conventional gear version or the Volpar-designed tricycle gear installation that was installed at the Beech factory. Eventually, only the tricycle-gear model was built. The last of nearly 8,000 Beechcraft Model 18s were delivered on November 26, 1969 when three Model Super H18 departed Beech Field for Japan, to be used by Japan Air Lines as multi-engine pilot trainers. A total of 149 H18 were produced from 1963-1970. (Refer to Appendix C, #7)

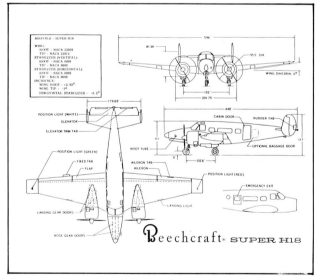

Instrument panel of Model Super H18 shows autopilot mode controller, weather radar installation. Panel had ample room for modern avionics equipment.

Beech considered construction of the Model 20M twin-engine version of the Model 17 in mid-1937, powered by two Menasco C6S4 Super Buccaneer, inverted, liquid-cooled 6-cylinder powerplants developing 260 hp each at 2300 rpm. Maximum speed was expected to be 240 mph, gross weight 4,850 pounds, range of 600 statute miles. Wingspan: 32 feet; length: 26 feet 9 inches. The Model 18 took precedence over the Model 20M; development ceased in 1938. ➤

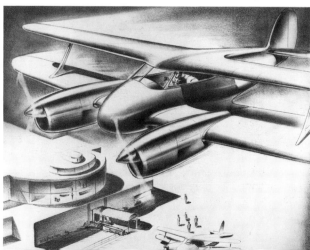

MODEL 23 MUSKETEER (PROTOTYPE)

Beech Aircraft Corporation entered the light, single-engine market in 1963 with the Model 23 Musketeer. Designed and developed at Wichita, the prototype Model 23 made its first flight 10-23-61 with S.C. Tuttle at the controls. Soon after the maiden flight, full-swiveling nose gear unit was moved forward and first flew on December 19, 1961. John I. Elliot was chief project engineer on the Model 23, which took advantage of Beech's manufacturing experience with truss-grid, honeycomb core material used to build control surfaces for the Convair F-106 jet fighter. The laminar flow wing used honeycomb ribs bonded to the external skin for drag reduction and strength. Musketeer prototype N948B is illustrated with nose gear in original, aft location.

MODEL 23 MUSKETEER

Beechcraft's new Musketeer featured trailing beam-type, tricycle landing gear and room for four occupants in a cabin surrounded with generous window area. Large, aft-curving windshield permitted excellent pilot visibility in all directions. Production Musketeers had the nose gear unit located further forward than prototype and the gear was made steerable through the rudder pedals to improve ground handling characteristics. Fuel capacity totalled 60 gallons, maximum gross weight was 2,300 pounds. Maximum speed 144 mph with a maximum range of 873 statute miles at 65% power setting. Powered by a four-cylinder, 160 hp Lycoming 0-320-D2B opposed engine, Model 23 sold for $13,300 including a single radio and complete flight instrumentation. Initial deliveries began in October, 1962 from the Wichita factory. 553 were produced in the 1963 model year. Note baggage door located on right side of fuselage.

MODEL A23-A23A-A23-24

Beech introduced the improved Model A23 Musketeer II in June, 1964 that featured a third cabin window, 165 hp fuel-injected Lycoming engine and minor interior/exterior refinements to enhance customer appeal. Price was $14,250. 346 Musketeer II were built, followed in 1965 by the new Musketeer III series that offered three different airplanes: 150 hp Sport III ($11,500); 165 hp Custom III ($14,950) and 200 hp Super III ($16,350). The four-place Model A23-24 Musketeer Super III first flew 11-19-65. Powered by a 200 hp Lycoming IO-360-A2B engine equipped with a two-blade, fixed-pitch propeller, maximum speed was 158 mph and normal category gross weight was 2,550 pounds. The Model A23A Musketeer Custom III used Lycoming's IO-346-A engine producing 165 hp at 2700 rpm and seated four. Model A23A first flight was 10-15-65. In 1966, Beech offered the six-seat Musketeer Custom III powered by a 180 hp Lycoming O-360-A2G. Maximum speed was 151 mph with a 860 statute mile range with 45 minute reserve. Model A23, A23A and A23-24 were produced at Beech's Liberal, Kansas facility that began manufacturing operations exclusively for the Musketeer series in June, 1964. Beech offered an optional left side cabin door on all models. Only the right door was standard. A 1966 Model A23-24 Musketeer Custom III is illustrated.

Musketeer instrument panel was well equipped for 1966 with dual nav/com radios, ADF, gyroscopic flight instruments and exhaust gas temperature (EGT) system.

MODEL A23-19 SPORT/MODEL B19 SPORT 150

Beech introduced the two-place, Model A23-19 Sport in 1965 as an economy version of the A23-series used for basic flight training. Powered by a 150 hp Lycoming 0-320-E2C series engine, the A23-19 had a maximum speed of 140 mph and a gross weight of 2,250 pounds. Only two cabin windows were installed, reminiscent of the early Model 23 Musketeer. In 1968 the Model 19A Musketeer Sport III aerobatic version was offered, delivered with g-meter, quick-release right-side door and shoulder harnesses as standard equipment. In 1969, the Musketeer Custom III received an aerobatic version with a 180 hp Lycoming engine. The Model B19 debuted in 1970 followed in 1972 by the B-19 Sport 150, both with 150 hp Lycoming powerplants. Production of the Model A23/19/19A/M19A/B19 occurred from 1966 to 1978 and totalled 1,525 airplanes. Model B19 Sport 150 is illustrated.

MODEL A24R/B24R/C24R

In 1970, Beech engineers designed the Model A24R Super R featuring an electro-hydraulic, retractable landing gear system. Main gear retracted outward into large recesses while the nose gear rotated 90 degress to lay flat in its well. A Lycoming IO-360-A1B, fuel-injected engine developing 200 hp at 2700 rpm powered the A24R to a cruising speed of 162 mph at 7,500 feet. 60 gallons of fuel permitted a range of 711 statute miles at 75 % power setting. Price was $24,950. In 1972, Beech introduced the B24R, named "Sierra 200" with standard left side cabin door and built 55 airplanes that year. The B24R featured system and interior refinements, including a 1 1/2-inch lower instrument panel and improved IO-360-A2B engine with counter-weighted crankshaft, relocated oil cooler (firewall). Built from 1973 to 1976, 299 B24R were produced. In 1977, the C24R Sierra 200 entered production beginning with c/n MC-499 and continuing through MC-795 for a total of 345 airplanes. C24 featured fairings to reduce drag around main gear, aileron gap seals and improved, more efficient propeller that gave a six-knot increase in speed and higher service ceiling. C24R illustrated banks away to show retracted gear.

MODEL B23/C23

The 1966 Model A23A Musketeer Custom III evolved into the Model B23 Musketeer Custom III of 1968 and Model C23 of 1970. Major changes for the 1970 model year included a wider front cabin (4 1/2 inches added at the two front seats) and larger, reshaped cabin windows. Two windows were standard on the B19 Sport, three on the Custom and Super models while the Super could add a fourth window when the optional third seat was ordered (making the Musketeer Super a six-seat airplane). First C23 was c/n M-1285 and continued through M-1361 in 1971. Seating four, the C23 received a 180 hp Lycoming 0-360-A4G engine in 1972 and featured a standard left side door. Renamed Sundowner 180, maximum cruising speed was 143 mph and gross weight 2,450 pounds. The first production Sundowner 180 was c/n M-1362 and the last was M-2392, built in 1983. The instrument panel on the 1973 Sport and Sundowner was lowered 1 1/2 inches for improved forward visibility and the throttle, mixture and carburetor heat controls were mounted in a new quadrant. Only significant change for 1974 was a one inch increase in window height. Late-model C23 series (1975-1983) have Avco Lycoming 0-360-A2G, 0-360-A4G, 0-360-A4J or 0-360-A4K engines developing 180 hp at 2700 rpm. Model C23 Sundowner 180 illustrated has optional heated pitot tube on left wing, Beech Aero Club insignia on wing and tail.

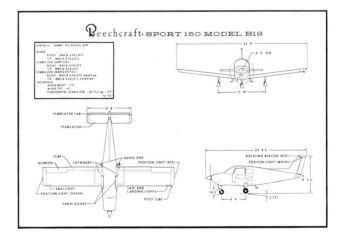

1977 Sundowner instrument panel features digital display nav/comm avionics, transponder and complete instrumentation for IFR flight.

MODEL 25/26 WICHITA

Designed by Beech engineers under the supervision of Ted Wells, the Beechcraft Model 25 answered the U.S. Army's need for an advanced multi-engine pilot trainer that could be built with non-strategic materials, primarily wood. Development began in early 1940 and cost $255,000. The prototype crashed and burned on May 5, 1941 during army tests. Undaunted, Beech initiated design work for the followup Model 26 on May 6, 1941. On July 19 the new AT-10 made its first flight with Beech test pilot H.C. "Ding" Rankin and co-pilot John P. Gaty at the controls. Deliveries began in February, 1942 and 748 were manufactured that year. Beech production ceased in 1943 after a total of 1,771 AT-10 were built.

The Globe Aircraft Corporation produced 600 ships before terminating production in 1944 for a total of 2,371 AT-10 built in World War Two. Majority of fuselage and wings were constructed of plywood with sheet aluminum used only in the cockpit/nose sections, nacelles and cowlings. Subcontractors provided majority of AT-10 parts, components and subassemblies because they could be manufactured by relatively unskilled labor. Powered by two 290 hp Lycoming R-680-9 radial engines with two-blade, constant-speed propellers, AT-10 had a maximum speed of 190 mph. Cockpit canopy slid aft for entry/exit. AT-10 served alongside Cessna's AT-17 "Bobcat" advanced pilot trainer, also designed to the same basic specifications, during the war.

Model 26/AT-10, second prototype built, November, 1941. Wood fuselage was covered by doped fabric.

AT-10 "Wichita" advanced multi-engine trainers await students.

Early production AT-10 advanced, multi-engine trainers fly in formation. Beech produced a total of 1,771 AT-10s during the war. (Jim Horne collection).

View of busy Beechcraft assembly line shows a portion of the 1,771 AT-10 trainers produced from 1941 to 1943. (Jim Horne collection).

MODEL 28

Beechcraft's Model 28 was designed as a ground attack aircraft capable of delivering knock-out blows to fortified gun emplacements, armored vehicles and coastal surface vessels. A hand-picked engineering team led by Bill Cassidy began development in 1943, and the first airplane flew on May 7, 1944 with Beech test pilot Vern Carstens at the wheel. The Model 28 was not a modified Model 18 but a totally new design. Designated XA-38 "Grizzly" by the U.S. Army Air Force (but also known as the "Destroyer" at Beech), a 75 mm Type T15E1 automatic cannon with 20 rounds was mounted in the nose. Aiming the cannon was simple: point the airplane at the target and fire. Sighting was aided by a Type N-6 reflector unit. Six .50-caliber machine guns complemented the cannon's firepower. Four were located in twin,

remote-control turrets and two more in the lower nose section. A gunner controlled the turrets but the pilot could fire the lower turret and nose guns plus the cannon simultaneously if desired. Two, 2,300 hp Wright Duplex "Cyclone" GR-3350-43 18-cylinder, twin-row radial engines powered the XA-38 to a maximum speed of 331 mph at sea level. Basic gross weight was 29,900 pounds with a combat gross weight (with ordnance) of 36,332 pounds. Fuel capacity was 825 gallons in self-sealing tanks. "Grizzly" could carry bombs, chemical tanks, napalm and even torpedoes. Only two XA-38 were built, Army s/n 314406 and 314407, with 314406 delivered to the Army at Wright Field on July 7, 1945. Both airplanes were scrapped after the war. Wingspan was 67.08 feet, length 51.7 feet. XA-38 illustrated shows gunner's control compartment aft, top turret and 75 mm nose cannon.

AT-10 utilized for flight tests of V-tail configuration in 1944-1945 at the Beech factory.

Closeup view of XA-38 engines and 75 mm nose-mounted cannon.

Instrument panel of 1961 Model 35-A33 Debonair, c/n CD-330, N252AA. Magneto switch is between throttle and propeller control.

MODEL 35-33 DEBONAIR

Beech developed the Debonair to compete primarily with the new, high performance airplanes like Piper's Commanche and Cessna's Model 182. Priced at $19,995 (standard airplane) the four-place Debonair was intended to be distinctly different than its cousin, the Model 35 Bonanza, yet retain traditional Beechcraft quality and performance. A conventional empennage assembly was used that immediately set the Debonair apart from the Model 35. First flown on September 14, 1959, the new Beechcraft featured a very spartan interior and only exterior trim paint. When introduced in November, 1959, initial interest was strong and 233 airplanes were built the first year. Dealer acceptance was good, but Beech salesmen soon found it hard to sell the Debonair against the competition, not because of price or quality but because the airplane's general appearance and interior appointments were too basic and utilitarian. Powered by a six-cylinder, fuel-injected 225 hp Continental IO-470-J engine swinging a two-blade, constant-speed Hartzell propeller, the Model 35-33 had a maximum speed of 195 mph at sea level and a gross weight of 2,900 pounds. Debonair illustrated is c/n CD-1, N831R, Model 33-35 prototype.

MODEL 35-B33 DEBONAIR

The Model 35-B33 was produced from late 1961 through 1964, and received further refinements found on the production Model 35 Bonanza. A new instrument panel was installed (same as P35 Bonanza), a small fairing added to the vertical stabilizer, the front seat backs were adjustable, a stall warning horn replaced the light used on previous models and the N35 Bonanza leading edge fuel tanks offered 80 gallon capacity as an option. Exterior paint scheme was more sophisticated and landing gear extension speed increased to 165 mph. A total of 426 35-B33 were built. 1961 priced was $21,975 but increased to $23,500 in February, 1963. Engine remained 225 hp IO-470-K. B33 N829B is illustrated. Note mannequin in full business suit seated behind pilot.

MODEL 35-A33 DEBONAIR

Beech revised the Debonair in 1961 to make it more appealing to potential customers. Overall exterior paint was made standard, interior features such as sun visors, seat padding, chart box and small hat shelf were added. A33 c/n started with CD-251 and 154 were built. CD-251 -CD-300 equipped with Continental 225 hp IO-470-J. CD-301 and after had IO-470-K of 225 hp. Gross weight was 3,000 pounds and maximum speed 195 mph. Price increased to $21,750. Debonair illustrated has optional heated pitot tube.

MODEL 35-C33 DEBONAIR

1965 Model 35-C33 incorporated changes that made it more like the Model 35 Bonanza. The dorsal fairing was extended forward, a larger, third cabin window was optional and the aft seats were mounted on individual tracks and featured adjustable backs. Four-color exterior paint scheme and the Bonanza's cabin assist step were also standard. Gross weight increased 50 pounds to 3,050. 305 35-C33 were produced from 1965-1967. Service ceiling was 17,800 feet, standard fuel capacity 50 gallons (80 gallons optional).

MODEL 35-C33A DEBONAIR

In 1966, Beech offered the 285 hp 35-C33A equipped with Continental IO-520-B engine. Distinguished from the C33 version by its exterior paint scheme, the C33A was developed to compete with Piper's 250 hp Commanche and to allow owners of older model Debonairs to step up in horsepower and performance. Maximum

speed was 208 mph. A one-piece windshield improved overall appearance and became standard on all subsequent Debonair models. The engine installation was the same as the Model S35 Bonanza: canted down two degrees and right 2 1/2 degrees to reduce rudder force during takeoff and climb. Price was $29,875; later increased to $31,000.

MODEL D33 (EXPERIMENTAL)

In 1965, the U.S. Air Force experimented with a modified Model S35, c/n D-7859, N5847K, for possible application as a light, ground attack aircraft. A conventional tail was installed and the designation changed to Model D33. A variety of ordnance could be carried, including 250-pound napalm bombs, 272-pound general purpose (GP) bombs, 7.62 mm miniguns and 2.75-inch unguided rockets. Six wing hardpoints were provided, the inboard points stressed for 600 pounds and the outboard points stressed for 300 pounds. Tests were conducted at Eglin AFB, Florida. (Courtesy Larry A. Ball)

MODEL PD 249 (EXPERIMENTAL)

An improved version of c/n D-7859, PD 249 was evaluated by USAF for further investigations of the airplane's ground attack capabilities. A 350 hp Continental GIO-520 was installed for more power and a three-blade propeller was added. Wing hardpoints remained unchanged. Although tests were promising, the Air Force did not pursue extended development of the PD 249 and the project was cancelled in the early 1970s. PD 249 is illustrated with ordnance on all six wing hardpoints and overall three-tone camouflage scheme. (Courtesy Larry A. Ball).

MODEL E33 BONANZA

In the 1968 model year, the Debonair became a Bonanza in name only, although both models were very similar in appearance, appointments and performance. Equipped with a 225 hp Continental IO-470 engine, the E33 had a maximum speed of 195 mph at sea level, carried 50 gallons of fuel in standard tanks (80-gallon tanks optional), and had a sea level rate of climb of 930 feet per minute. Gross weight: 3,050 pounds. Useful load: 1,188 pounds. The third cabin window, optional on earlier Debonairs, was made standard on the E33. A total of 116 Model E33 Bonanzas were produced in 1968-1969 model years. Price: $31,750. Note the new, larger "Speed Sweep" windshield introduced by Beech on the 1968 Model 33 and 35 Bonanzas.

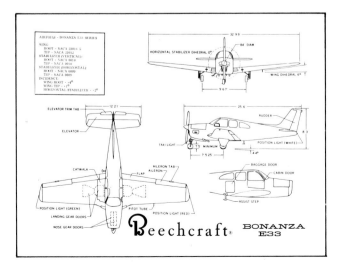

MODEL E33A BONANZA

Offered in the 1968-1969 model years, the Model. E33A was identical to the E33 except for its 285 hp Continental IO-520-B powerplant. Maximum speed increased to 208 mph, sea level rate of climb was 1,200 feet per minute with a service ceiling of 18,300 feet. Beech included a Mark 12A nav/com radio as standard equipment, later changed to the solid-state Mark 16 unit. Price: $35,750. 79 E33A were produced in 1968-1969. (Courtesy Larry A. Ball)

MODEL E33B/E33C

Aerobatic versions of the E33 and E33A, the Model E33B and E33C were very similar except for customer choice of engines. The E33B had 225 hp, the E33C had 285 hp and became the preferred type; no E33B were produced. Both models were licensed in the acrobatic category at 2,800 pounds gross weight or could operate at their full 3,300-pound maximum gross weight in the utility category. Primary structural changes to the standard E33-series were Queen Air aileron ribs; horizontal stabilizer used Travel Air front and rear spars; heavier gauge skin thickness on vertical stabilizer leading edge; larger rudder cables and additional stringers in aft fuselage section. 25 Model E33C were built. Price: $38,250. During aerobatic flight, only the two front seats were occupied and a quick-release door was standard equipment, along with front seat shoulder harnesses, a g-meter and special fuel boost pump and unique checkerboard paint on wing and tail tips. Typical aerobatic maneuvers approved were aileron roll, barrel roll, inside loop, Immelman, Cuban eight and split-S. Two Model E33C are illustrated. (Courtesy Larry A. Ball)

MODEL F33 BONANZA

The 1970 Model F33 Bonanza was actually a refined Model E33, still using the Continental IO-470-K of 225 hp. F33 had restyled third cabin window of the Model V35B, "Speed Sweep" windshield, three gear down annunciator lights, redesigned subpanels and switches, a lower glareshield and Hartwell quick-opening latches for the engine cowling. Empty weight increased to 1,885 pounds, maximum gross weight was 3,050 pounds. Maximum speed remained at 195 mph. Priced at $34,150 each, 20 Model F33 were produced, all in the 1970 model year.

MODEL F33A BONANZA

Two different versions of the F33A were built, the short-fuselage model produced in 1970 and the long-fuselage model built in 1971, featuring a 19-inch extension in the aft cabin section. 26 F33A were built with short fuselages. 34 were produced with the long fuselage, allowing two important benefits: a larger baggage door and six-seat configuration previously available only in the Model V35B Bonanza. The 1971 F33A possessed all of the V35B's glamour, both inside and out, with the only difference between airplanes being the choice of empennage design. Maximum speed was 208 mph at sea level, but the higher gross weight of 3,400 pounds decreased rate of climb to 1,136 feet per minute and service ceiling to 17,500 feet. Price of the short-cabin F33A was $38,150 while the long-cabin version cost $41,600. 1983 Model F33A Bonanza is illustrated.

MODEL F33C BONANZA

Five F33C aerobatic Bonanzas were built in 1970 and all were short-fuselage airplanes. No F33C were built in 1971-1972. From 1973 on, all Model F33C Bonanzas featured the 19-inch longer fuselage and the same structural features of the earlier Model E33C aerobatic Bonanza. Powered by a 285 hp Continental IO-520-BB engine, the F33A seated four or five with optional fifth seat. Maximum gross weight: 3,400 pounds; useful load: 1,248 pounds. 23 F33C were built in 1986, including 21 for the Mexican Air Force: c/n CJ-156-CJ-176. Mexican Air Force F33C is illustrated, flown by Beech production flight test pilot Gale McKinney. Note vortex generators on wing leading edge. 1987 Model F33C cost $184,500 at the factory.

MODEL G33 BONANZA

Beech created the 1972 Model G33 Bonanza by taking the Model F33 and installing a 260 hp Continental IO-470-N powerplant. Only 50 G33 were built before production ended in 1973. Gross weight: 3,300 pounds. Price: $41,450. 1972 G33 had the improved interior configuration of the 1972 Model V35B Bonanza. Maximum speed: 204 mph. Range with 80 gallons of fuel (optional tanks): 1,243 statute miles. (Courtesy Larry A. Ball)

MODEL 34 TWIN-QUAD

The postwar feeder airline market look promising in 1945 and Beech Aircraft Corporation forged ahead with design of the Model 34 Twin-Quad, intended to fulfill the requirements of upstart and established feeder operators. The novel propulsion arrangement of two engines (with individual clutch assemblies) in each wing driving a single propeller through a common gearbox was designed by Beech engineer Alex Odevseff. Engineers W.A. Day, J.W. Massey and W.O. Stephens also contributed their talents to the Model 34 project. Featuring a large, V-tail empennage, the 20-passenger, high-wing Beechcraft made its first flight in October, 1947 from Beech Field. Powered by four, eight-cylinder Lycoming geared, supercharged, opposed GSO-580 engines developing 400 hp each at 3300 rpm,

the Twin-Quad could carry 1,000 pounds of express cargo and had a range of 1,400 statute miles with 45 minute fuel reserves while cruising at 180 mph. Although the airplane was designed for a maximum speed of 300 mph, that figure was never attained during the more than 200 hours of extensive flight testing accomplished from October, 1947 to January, 1949. Wingspan was 70 feet, length 53 feet and height to top of the V-tail nearly 18 feet. Maximum design gross weight was 20,000 pounds. Fuselage keel was designed to withstand gear-up landing loads and one unintentional landing incident demonstrated that the airplane could survive such an occurrence with minimal damage. The prototype (NX90521) made a forced landing on January 17, 1949 shortly after takeoff and was damaged beyond economical repair. (Refer to Appendix C, #8)

In-flight view of Model 34 Twin Quad over Wichita, Kansas.

Model 34 Twin Quad after intentional belly landing test. ▼

Beech engineers, technicians and Walter Beech pose with Model 34 Twin Quad engine test stand setup. Mr. Beech is sixth from left. The engines used for gearbox/clutch testing were surplus, 450 hp, six-cylinder Lycoming units with a design life of 50 hours.

MODEL 35 BONANZA

A legend in its own right, the Beechcraft Model 35 Bonanza flew for the first time on December 22, 1945 with veteran Beech test pilot Vern L. Carstens at the wheel. The Bonanza met Walter H. Beech's demand for an airplane that would carry four people and their baggage in car-like comfort at 180 mph. Five engineers were assigned by Ted Wells to design the Model 35. Ralph Harmon led the team composed of Noel Naidenoff, Alex Odevseff, Jerry Gordon and Wilson Erhart (all but Erhart are known to have worked on the challenging XA-38 "Grizzly" project in 1944-1945). Certification was granted on March 25, 1947 and production of the first version, the Model 35, occurred in 1947-1948. 1,500 were built, more than any other Bonanza model. Powered by a 165 hp Continental E-165 opposed engine, the "straight 35" had a range of 750 statute miles on 40 gallons of fuel. Later production Model 35s had E-185-1 engines developing 185 hp for one minute at 2300 rpm, 165 hp continuous. Gross weight was 2,550 pounds. Price: $7,975 from c/n D-1 - c/n D-973, then increased to $8,945 from c/n D-974 - c/n D-1500. Model 35 illustrated was built in March, 1947. Famous V-tail was mounted at 30 degrees from horizontal. Tricycle gear was electrically operated and rugged enough for unimproved landing fields. The nose gear was not steerable on original Model 35 Bonanzas. Wood propeller featured controllable pitch but no governor device.

MODEL A35 BONANZA

Built in 1949, the Model A35 Bonanza was the first to incorporate a box-type, sheet metal spar carrythrough that replaced the tubular design used in the 1947-1948 airplanes and it was the first Bonanza to be licensed in the Utility category at full gross weight of 2,650 pounds. A total of 701 A35 were produced. Other changes were: gear down speed increased from 105 mph to 125 mph; flap extended speed increased to 105 mph; steerable nosewheel installation; useful load increased to 1,070 pounds. Model A35 illustrated has optional overall exterior paint scheme and was the 2,000th Model 35 built.

MODEL B35 BONANZA

The Model B35 Bonanza had all the improvements found in the A35 but featured the Continental E-185-8 engine that developed 196 hp for one minute at 2450 rpm. Priced at $11,975, 480 B35 were produced during the 1950 sales year. Flap extension increased from 20 to 30 degrees, front and rear cabin armrests and chart pockets were minor improvements found on the Model B35. B35 illustrated has standard exterior paint scheme. Note baggage door located on right side.

◄   MODEL 35 BONANZA "WAIKIKI BEECH"

Captain William Odom's famous record transoceanic flight was made in March, 1949 flying Beechcraft Model 35 Bonanza c/n D-4. Man and machine flew 4,957 miles nonstop from Hickam Field, Territory of Hawaii to Teterboro Airport in northern New Jersey. Flying time was 36 hours, 2 minutes. Odom is shown in this photograph with c/n D-4 after the historic flight. As of 1987, the airplane was on display in the National Air and Space Museum in Washington, D.C.

1948 Model 35 Bonanza in optional overall paint scheme.

1948 Model 35 Bonanza instrument panel. Note color-coded arcs and radial lines on airspeed indicator required on all civil aircraft after 1946. Top of white arc for flap extension is 100 mph.

1950 Model C35 instrument panel shows refinement in instrument and control placement. Note flat, energy-absorbing control wheel first installed on Model B35 Bonanza.

MODEL C35/D35/E35 BONANZA

The Model C35 Bonanza was built from late 1950 through the 1952 sales year. Significant changes included a more powerful Continental E-185-11 developing 185 hp continuous and 205 hp at takeoff for one minute. Chord of the V-tail was increased 20% and the V-angle increased to 33 degrees. Gross weight was 2,700 pounds and maximum speed 190 mph. 719 C35 were manufactured and were priced at $12,990 initially but increased to $18,990 in 1952. Model D35 of 1952 had new exterior paint scheme and 298 were produced. D35 sold for $18,990. 1954 Model E35 Bonanza offered two engines: E-185-11 of 185 hp continuous or the new Continental E-225-8 developing 225 hp at takeoff for one minute at 2450 rpm. Model E35 cost $18,990 with E-185-11, $19,990 with E-225-8 engine. 1951 Model C35 is illustrated. Note retracted assist step.

MODEL F35 - MODEL M35 BONANZA

Beech added a third cabin window to the 1955 Model F35 Bonanza along with heavier aluminum skin thickness on the wing leading edges and strengthening of the V-tail spar cap. F35 was available with E-185-11 or E-225-8 engine and most customers preferred the higher horsepower E-225-8. 392 Model F35 were built and cost $19,990 with the 225 hp Continental. The 1956 Model G35 featured the E-225-8 as standard equipment, gross weight was 2,775 pounds gear extension speed increased to 140 mph. Windshield thickness increased to 1/4 inch. 476 G35 were produced. Price was $21,990. Model H35 of 1957 featured new 240 hp O-470-G engine, Model 50 Twin Bonanza wing spar caps and leading edge skin of reduced thickness and V-tail spar caps and elevators were strengthened. 464 Model H35 were manufactured, priced at $22,650 each. In 1958, the Model J35 was the first fuel-injected Bonanza, using Continental's 250 hp IO-470-C and cost $24,300. 396 Model J35 were built. The Model K35 Bonanza was first to have 50 gallon fuel capacity and optional fifth seat in aft cabin. Gross weight was 2,950 pounds. A total of 436 Model K35 were manufactured in the 1959 sales year. K35 cost $25,300. Maximum speed: 210 mph. There were no significant changes to the 1960 Model M35 Bonanza except for a new wingtip design. 400 M35 were produced. 1956 Model G35 is illustrated.

190 mph Model F35 Bonanza flies over Wichita, Kansas.

MODEL N35/P35 BONANZA

Beech revamped the already classic Bonanza in 1961 by adding a new, larger third cabin window and installing a 260 hp Continental IO-470-N engine in the Model N35. Gross weight increased to 3,125 pounds but the extra weight caused rate of climb to decrease from the Model M35's 1,170 fpm (feet per minute) to 1,150 fpm. 280 Model N35 Bonanzas were produced. Price was $26,500. The 1962

Model P35 Bonanza had a completely redesigned instrument panel featuring avionics mounted to the right of center panel, new subpanels and all flight instruments were shock-mounted in a separate, hinged panel in front of the pilot. 467 Model P35 were built. Price: $27,650. Model N35 Bonanza illustrated shows fixed assist step first installed on Model N35.

MODEL S35 BONANZA

Produced in the 1964-1965 model year, the Model S35 Bonanza's fuselage length was increased 19 inches allowing six occupants to be seated in the cabin when optional fifth/sixth seats were installed. The third cabin window was reshaped and Continental's IO-520-B engine brought 285 hp to the Bonanza for the first time. The fuel-injected powerplant was mounted in a redesigned cradle that was canted down 2 degrees and right 2 1/2 degrees to reduce rudder forces during takeoff and climb. The S35 Bonanza was also the fastest built up to that time, with a maximum speed of 212 mph. A total of 667 Model S35 were built. Price: $28,750.

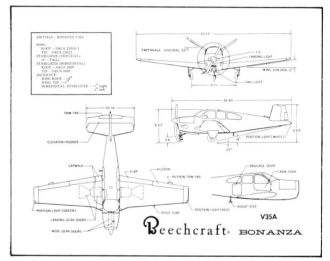

1956 Model G35 Bonanza instrument panel shows padded glareshield and center-mounted engine instrument cluster.

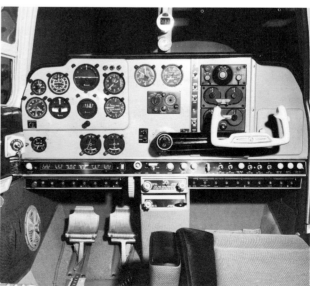

Model S35 Bonanza instrument panel illustrates new design first installed on the Model P35. Subpanels house switches, avionics are mounted within reach of either front seat occupant.

MODEL V35/V35A BONANZA

Beech introduced the Model V35 Bonanza in 1966, powered with the 285 hp Continental IO-520-B that gave a maximum speed of 210 mph at sea level. Gross weight was 3,400 pounds. There were few changes from the Model S35 Bonanza, the most salient being a one-piece windshield. Price was $32,500. 543 Model V35 Bonanzas were produced in 1966-1967. In 1968, the Model V35A featured the new "Speed-Sweep" windshield of increased area. The leading edge of the windshield was mounted six inches farther

forward than previous Bonanzas and possessed 12 degrees more slope angle. A total of 426 Model V35A were built. In 1968 Beech renamed the Debonair "Bonanza" and all subsequent Model 35s were denoted by the prefix "V", with each derivative version identified by a suffix letter. The 1968 V35A was the first Bonanza to adopt the new classification system. Maximum speed: 210 mph; service ceiling: 17,500 feet. Price: $36,850. 1966 Model V35 Bonanza is illustrated. Note fixed assist step.

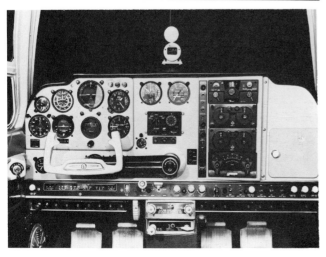

Beechcraft **BONANZA V35B**

MODEL V35TC/V35A-TC/V35B-TC BONANZA

Beech developed the turbocharged Model V35TC in 1966 when turbocharging and high altitude flying were becoming more commonplace for general aviation airplanes. Using the Continental 285 hp TSIO-520-D, the V35TC could maintain full rated power up to 19,000 feet where it had a maximum speed of 250 mph. Priced at $37,750, 79 V35TC were produced in 1966-1967. Oxygen system and electro-thermal propeller deice were two popular options for the Model V35TC Bonanza. For 1968-1969 model years, the Model V35A-TC incorporated the "Speed-Sweep" windshield and other improvements found on the naturally-aspirated Model V35A. A total of 46 Model V35A-TC were built. Price: $42,750. The last turbocharged Beechcraft Bonanza until the Model A36TC of 1979 was the 1970 Model V35B-TC. Only seven were produced. Three gear down annunciator lights were standard, Baron-type fuel gauges were installed and Hartwell quick-release cowling latches were employed. Powered by a 285 hp TSIO-520-D powerplant, The V35B-TC's maximum speed was 250 mph at 19,000 feet with a cruise speed of 230 mph at 24,000 feet, full throttle/2500 rpm. Model V35B-TC was not produced in 1971. 1966 Model V35TC Bonanza is illustrated.

1966 Model V35 Bonanza instrument panel.

MODEL V35B BONANZA

1970 was the first year for the Model V35B Bonanza. Only minor changes were implemented, including three gear down annunciator lights, anti-slosh fuel bladder cells and new interior styling. 218 V35B were produced in 1970. Price: $41,600. The 1972 Model V35B received a major interior redesign that required structural changes to the upper cabin sections. More durable materials were employed and the overhead fresh air ventilation system was improved. Price was $41,600 and 104 were built in 1972. In 1978 the V35B received a 24-volt electrical system, 4-second gear retraction/extension time. Beech built the 10,000th Model 35

Bonanza, c/n D-10000, on February 9, 1977. The airplane was flown on a nationwide tour to celebrate the Model 35's 30-year dominance of the high performance, single-engine market. The last Model 35 built was V35B c/n D-10403, delivered to Beech production flight test department on November 11, 1982 and delivered to a Beech dealer in May, 1984. Last Model 35 delivered to a retail customer was V35B c/n D-10399, delivered in August, 1984. Model V35B N35YR, painted to celebtrate 35 years of Bonanza production in 1982, is illustrated flown by Beech production test pilot Bob Buettgenbach.

MODEL O35 BONANZA (EXPERIMENTAL)

Beech built the Model O35 Bonanza in 1961 as an experimental testbed featuring a laminar flow wing with integral (wet) fuel cells in the leading edge, replacing rubber bladder tanks. The tricycle landing gear was modified with trailing beam-type main gear assemblies and new gear doors. The nose gear remained unchanged. A 260 hp Continental IO-470-N engine powered the O35. Despite the advantage of increased fuel capacity, wingtip fuel filler access and smoother landing gear operation, the O35 was not developed beyond the experimental stage. (Courtesy Larry A. Ball)

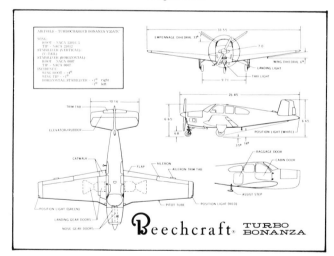

Model V35B instrument panel with engine instrument cluster at center, flight instruments on shock-mounted panel, subpanel switches/autopilot mode controller at left and circuit breakers on right subpanel.

MODEL 36/A36 BONANZA

Based on the 1968 Model E33 Bonanza, Beech's Model 36 was created by moving the E33A's aft cabin bulkhead back 19 inches and adding a 10-inch section to the fuselage. The wing was relocated aft, placing pilot and passengers 10 inches farther forward on the wing, thereby increasing the CG range and stability of the airplane. Two outward-opening doors were installed on the right fuselage side that permitted easy passenger or cargo loading and unloading. The doors could be removed for flight. Powered by a 285 hp Continental IO-520 engine, maximum speed was 204 mph and the Model 36 was licensed in the Utility category at its maximum gross weight of 3,600 pounds. An immediate success when introduced in June, 1968, the Model 36 was primarily aimed at the air taxi or light cargo market. Three interiors were offered: standard, utility and a deluxe design. Priced at $40,650, 105 were built in 1968 and 79 in 1969. In 1970 Beech added a more luxurious interior similar to the Model V35B, three gear down annunciator lights, Hartwell quick-release cowling latches and redesigned instrument subpanels to create the Model A36 Bonanza. Redesigned wing tips changed span from 32 feet 10 inches on the Model 36 to 33 feet six inches on the A36. 56 were built in 1970 and 42 in 1971. In 1972 electrically-operated, vertical-readout engine instruments were standard and in 1978 a 24-volt electrical system and 4-second gear retraction/extension time were incorporated, beginning with A36 c/n E-1111. A major change occurred in 1984 when Beech completely redesigned the instrument panel. Separate shaft-type control wheels, circular, vertically-stacked engine instruments were mounted on the new instrument panel that was canted back at the top for easier pilot scanning, and quadrant-mounted throttle/propeller/mixture controls were installed. Small, wedge-like vortex generators were added to the outboard wing leading edge for improved roll control at high angle of attack. The engine changed to a 300 hp (takeoff and continuous) Continental IO-550-B. Takeoff gross weight increased to 3,650 pounds. 95 A36 were built in 1984. A36 illustrated is flown by Beech production test pilot (and three-time women's national aerobatic champion) Joyce Case. 1987 Model A36 Bonanza cost $207,150 fly away factory (FAF).

MODEL A36TC BONANZA

After a nine-year absence, Beech reentered the single-engine turbocharged market in 1979 with the Model A36TC Bonanza powered by a Continental TSIO-520-UB engine developing 300 hp. Beech engineers eliminated cowl flaps by designing a series of air cooling louvers that provided adequate airflow inside the engine compartment. The absence of cowl flaps was viewed as both a reduction in maintenance and pilot workload. The standard Model A36 Bonanza cabin heating system was revised to produce 20% more heat to keep cabin occupants warm during high altitude flights. The A36TC was a welcome addition to Beech's product line and 32 were produced the first year, from c/n EA-1 to c/n EA-32. Fuel capacity remained at 74 gallons useable and maximum certificated altitude was 25,000 feet. A36TC illustrated is c/n EA-1, N36TC, a company demonstrator.

MODEL B36TC BONANZA

Sales success with the Model A36TC led to the improved Model B36TC in 1981. Significant changes were incorporated into the turbocharged, six-seat Beechcraft, including a completely redesigned instrument panel with separate, shaft-type control wheels, quadrant-mounted throttle/propeller/mixture controls and circular, vertically-mounted engine instruments. Fuel capacity was increased to 108 gallons maximum (102 gallons useable) and wingspan increased from 33 feet, 6 inches (A36TC) to 37 feet, 10 inches. Wedge-like, vortex generators were installed on the wing leading edge to improve roll control at high angle of attack. Minor improvements were made to the engine/turbocharger installation and air conditioning was available as an option. Maximum takeoff gross weight increased to 3,850 pounds. Engine: Continental TSIO-520-UB rated at 300 hp (continuous). Cruise speed at maximum power (31 inches Hg manifold pressure/2400 rpm): 200 knots TAS (true airspeed), ISA conditions at 25,000 feet. B36TC c/n start at EA-242 and 50 were built in 1982, 65 in 1983. 1987 c/n start with EA-462. Price (1987): $233,250.

MODEL T36TC (EXPERIMENTAL)

Beech engineers modified a basic Model A36 Bonanza fuselage with newly-designed T-tail for experimental flight testing intended to investigate the feasability of a pressurized, single-engine Bonanza. Designated c/n EC-1 (N2065T) the T36TC was an unpressurized testbed powered by a 325 hp Continental TSIO-520 engine with aft-mounted turbocharger, requiring a 12-inch extension forward of the windshield to accomodate the powerplant. The T36TC made its first flight on February 16, 1979 with Beech engineering test pilots Lou Johansen and Robert Suter at the controls. A total of 82 hours, 45 minutes of testing were accumulated during 89 flights, with the last flight made on January 25, 1980. T36TC illustrated flown by Lou Johansen.

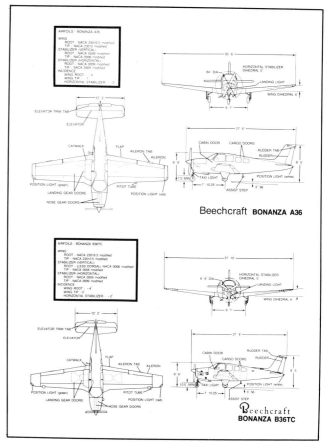

Beechcraft **BONANZA A36**

Beechcraft **BONANZA B36TC**

MODEL 1079 (MILITARY)

Built for the U.S. Air Force to perform electronic surveillance missions during the conflict in Southeast Asia, the Model 1079 was designated "Pave Eagle II" and were improved versions of the Model 1074 "Pave Eagle I" (highly modified Model E33A). Also known as QU-22B, the Model 1079 were Model A36 Bonanzas equipped with tip tanks for increased fuel capacity and endurance on station, 375 hp Continental engines with special reduction gearboxes to turn the propeller at a very low rpm for noise reduction. QU-22B was designed to be flown by remote control on missions with a pilot and observer on board to monitor equipment, but could also be hand-flown by the pilot if necessary. Note tip tanks and aft two cabin windows that are blanked out.

MODEL 45 MENTOR

First flown on December 2, 1948 by Beech test pilot Vern L. Carstens, the Model 45 Mentor originated as a private venture by Beech Aircraft Corporation to develop a basic trainer for military service. Featuring a full-vision, three-segment canopy over the two cockpits, the Mentor was based primarily on the commercial Model 35 Bonanza. Major departures from the Model 35 were a conventional empennage (Beech did consider a V-tail for the Model 45) and narrow fuselage. The prototype was powered by a Continental E-185 engine rated at 185 hp (takeoff), 165 hp continuous and had a maximum speed of 176 mph and a cruise speed of 160 mph at 10,000 feet. Gross weight was 2,650 pounds. Stressed for 10 positive and 4.5 negative G, the Mentor was tough and could perform all aerobatic maneuvers taught by most military services around the world. Model 45 illustrated is early prototype. Note general similarity to Model 35. ▼

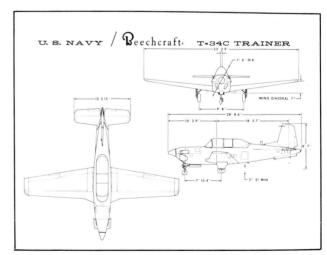

MODEL 45 - T-34A

The U.S. Air Force ordered three YT-34 in 1950 for service evaluation as a basic trainer. Satisfied with every aspect of the rough-and-ready Mentor, the air force ordered an initial production batch in 1953, designated T-34A. Two were delivered in September, 1953 and 88 were delivered by September, 1954. A total of 353 T-34A were built before production ended in October, 1956. The USAF received another 100 T-34A and the Royal Canadian Air Force (RCAF) took delivery of 25 Mentors built by the Canadian Car

and Foundry Co., Ltd of Fort William, Ontario after obtaining a manufacturing license from Beech in 1954. YT-34 was powered by a 220 hp Continental E-225-8 engine and had a maximum speed of 188 mph, cruised at 173 mph with a service ceiling of 20,000 feet. Gross weight was 2,950 pounds. USAF T-34A featured Continental O-470-13 engine rated at 225 hp giving a maximum speed of 189 mph. Gross weight was 2,950 pounds. YT-34 is illustrated during USAF evaluation.

MODEL 45 - T-34B

The U.S. Navy also purchased the Beechcraft Mentor for use as its primary trainer. After exhaustive operational evaluation the Navy started taking delivery of the T-34B in December, 1954. A total of 423 T-34B were produced for the U.S. Navy between October, 1954 and October, 1957 when the last 12 airplanes were delivered. Powered by a Continental O-470-13 engine developing 225 hp, the T-34B had a maximum speed of 188 mph and gross weight of 2,985 pounds. The Navy continued using the T-34B until the late 1970s when the turbine-powered Beech Model T-34C began to replace the aging trainers. Beech granted Model B45 Mentor (export version) production licenses to Japan in 1953 and Argentina in 1956. Fuji Heavy Industries built 137 for Japan's Air Self Defense Force (JASDF) and another 36 for the Philippine Air Force. Argentina assembled 75 Mentors in Cordoba for military service. Beech exported 318 Model B45. Total number of T-34's built between 1948-1958: 1,904. U.S. Navy T-34B is illustrated. ▼

Model 45 Mentor as T-34B for U.S. Navy evaluation. Note exhaust augmentor tubes.

MODEL T-34C/T-34C-1 TURBINE MENTOR

In 1972-1973, Beech reengineered the venerable Model T-34, transforming it into a powerful, economical and rugged turboprop trainer designated Model T-34C and Model T-34C-1. The U.S. Navy evaluated the T-34C version, powered by a Pratt & Whitney PT6A-25 engine of 400 shp (shaft horsepower) in 1973, and purchased 18 in 1975, to be followed over the next seven years by over 330 T-34C trainers. The Model T-34C-1, powered by a 550 shp version of Pratt & Whitney's PT6A-25 turboprop engine, was designed as an export trainer with light ground attack capabilities. Initial deliveries began in 1977 when the Ecuadorian Air Force accepted six of 14 T-34C-1. Peru, Morocco, Argentina and Indonesia also ordered Beechcraft Model T-34C-1 for their military services. Trio of T-34C-1 illustrated were delivered to Peru, Morocco and Ecuador. (Refer to T-44A for T-34C photograph)

1946 Beechcraft "Plainsman" automobile, built in mockup form only, featured air-cooled aircraft engine for power, electric drive for wheels, automatic air suspension, six-seat capacity. 2,200-pound car capitalized on aerodynamics for 25 mpg economy.

Fastback design and Bonanza-type doors that curved into roof, generous window area were salient features of Beech Plainsman. Crash protection was integral part of design. Anticipated selling price was about $5,000.

MODEL F90-1 KING AIR

Introduced in the 1983 model year, the Model F90-1 featured pitot-type engine cowl design that improved air intake characteristics, particularly at high altitude. Pratt & Whitney PT6A-135A turboprop powerplants replaced -135 engines of the F90 but were still rated at 750 shp. Wingspan: 45 feet 10 1/2 inches. Main and auxiliary fuel tanks in the wings hold 388 gallons (total) and the auxiliary tanks, located in the wing center section, hold up to 41 gallons of fuel. The first F90-1 was c/n LA-202 in 1983, and a total of 33 airplanes were built from 1983 to 1985. Last F90-1 produced was LA-236. F90-1 first flight (LA-91): January 5, 1981. Pilot: Vaughn Gregg. First production F90-1 test flight (LA-202): December 7, 1982. Pilot: Don Benes, Beech Production Flight Test Department. Price (1985): $1,723,500 fly away factory (FAF).

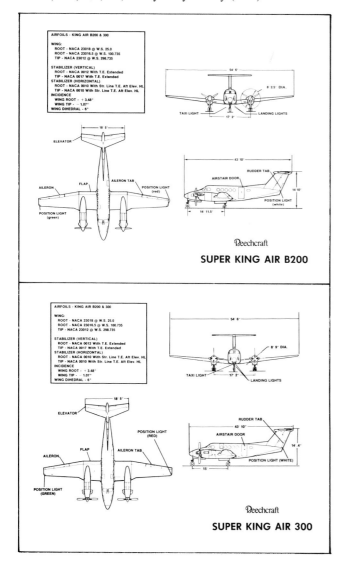

MODEL H90 - T-44A

The U.S. Navy awarded Beech Aircraft Corporation a contract in 1976 that eventually led to 61 Model H90 (not directly equivalent to Model C90 or E90 King Air) advanced, multi-engine pilot trainers designated T-44A. Powered by 550 shp PT6A-34B engines, performance was similar to Model C90 King Air. Maximum ramp weight: 9,710 pounds; maximum takeoff weight: 9,650 pounds. First deliveries occurred in 1977 and the majority of T-44A were assigned to Naval Air Station Corpus Christi, Texas. 13 T-44A were built in 1977: Beech c/n LL-1 - LL-13; Navy serial number s/n 160839 - 160851; 21 were built in 1978: c/n LL-14 - LL-35; Navy s/n 160852 - 160856 and s/n 160967 - 160983; 23 were produced in 1979: c/n LL-36 - LL-58; Navy s/n 160984 - 160986 and s/n 161057 - 161076. The last batch were manufactured in 1980: c/n LL-59 - LL-61; Navy s/n 161077 - 161079. T-44A illustrated flying formation with U.S. Navy T-34C.

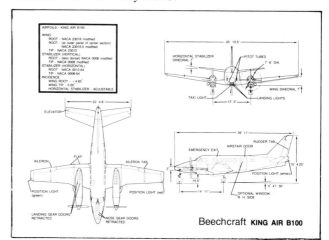

U.S. Army A100-1 (Beech Model 200) equipped for "Guardrail" duty.

MODEL 95 TRAVEL AIR

First flown on August 6, 1956 the Model 95 was designed to fill a gap between the single-engine Model 35 Bonanza and the much larger Model 50 Twin-Bonanza. Seating four in a cabin surrounded by generous window area, the Model 95 was powered by two, four-cylinder Lycoming 0-360-A1A engines developing 180 hp, swinging two-blade, constant-speed, full-feathering propellers. Maximum cruise speed was 200 mph, maximum speed 208 mph and gross weight 4,000 pounds. Service ceiling was 19,300 feet and two-engine rate of climb 1,350 feet per minute. With a fuel capacity of 112 gallons, the Model 95 could fly over 1,400 statute miles and maintained 8,000 feet on one engine at gross weight. Originally dubbed "Badger", the Model 95 had its name changed to "Travel Air" to avoid conflict with the U.S. Air Force, who had already assigned Badger as a code name for the Russian Tupolev TU-16 bomber (Beech was not aware of the military name). Wingspan was 37 feet 10 inches, length 25 feet four inches. 173 Model 95 were built in 1958, the airplane's first production year, followed by 128 in 1959. 1958 Model 95 is illustrated. Note baggage door on right side of fuselage and retracted assist step.

MODEL B95/B95A TRAVEL AIR

By 1960, after only two years of production, the Model 95 had established itself as one of the most popular light twin-engine airplanes available, and Beech introduced the B95 Travel Air to help ensure continued success. The cabin was lengthened 19 inches for more aft cabin room, the horizontal stabilizer and elevators received more area for improved pitch control and the vertical stabilizer incorporated a graceful dorsal fairing that improved overall appearance. Gross weight increased by 100 pounds to 4,100 while useful load went up to 1,465 pounds. Priced at $51,500 each, 150 B95 were built. The Model B95A debuted in 1961, boasting fuel-injected 180 hp Lycoming IO-360-B1A engines, and a higher maximum speed of 210 mph. 81 B95A were produced. Price at the factory was $49,500.

MODEL D95A TRAVEL AIR

The Model D95A Travel Air for 1963 received the same larger, curved third cabin window that was standard on the A55/B55 Baron. Forward baggage space in the redesigned, more tapered nose section was increased to 19 cubic feet, providing more room for the ever-increasing array of modern avionics available from Beech. Aft cabin baggage limit was increased to 400 pounds but price remained at $49,500. Like earlier Travel Airs, a combustion heater provided cabin heat and the tricycle landing gear was electrically operated. A total of 174 D95A were built.

MODEL E95 TRAVEL AIR

Beech produced only 14 Model E95 Travel Airs, all built in 1968. Minor refinement to the interior, a redesigned exterior paint scheme, new one-piece windshield and pointed propeller spinners were the most salient changes incorporated into one of Beech's most successful airplanes. Customer demand for the more powerful, affordable Model B55 Baron eroded Model E95's clientele and production ended in 1968 when the last 95, c/n TD-721, was built.

Model D95A Travel Air instrument panel. Note center-mounted throttles with mixture controls at right and propeller controls at left, throwover-type control wheel.

▼ MODEL 99/B99 AIRLINER

Beech airplanes such as the Model 18 and Model 70 Queen Airliner had long been used for charter and feeder airline service around the world, but in 1967 Beech unveiled the new Model 99 Airliner powered by two Pratt & Whitney PT6A-20 turboprop engines rated at 550 shp. An extended-fuselage Queen Air was used as a testbed to develop the airframe before turboprop powerplants were installed. The Model 99 seated 15 passengers and a crew of two or could be ordered in an executive version that seated six. A large, double cargo door was optional and often selected by airline operators. First flight of the long-fuselage prototype took place in December, 1965 and first flight with turboprop engines occurred in July, 1966. To accomodate the wide CG (center of gravity) range of the Model 99, the entire horizontal stabilizer was electrically trimmed by the pilot, with elevators acting in the conventional manner for pitch control. A standby electric trim system, geared to operate at 1/3 the speed of the main trim system, provided redundancy. Pulsed tones informed the crew anytime trim was occurring. 99 had a wingspan of 45 feet 10 1/2 inches, length of 44 feet 6 3/4 inches and a gross weight of 10,400 pounds. Maximum cruising speed was 284 mph with a range of 1,000 statute miles. Deliveries began in 1968, and most airplanes were delivered with the optional, removeable cargo pod that held an additional 600 pounds. In 1969 Beech delivered nine Model 99A with derated UACL PT6A-27 engines (550 shp) to the Chilean Air Force replacing its fleet of Beech C-45s. In 1972, the improved Model B99 began production, equipped with 680 shp PT6A-28 engines, 10,900-pound maximum takeoff weight and featuring airframe and systems improvements of the corporate Model A100 King Air. 101 Model 99 were built, 43 Model 99A and only one A99A, with special, decreased capacity fuel system. 18 Model B99 were produced but some 99 and 99A were converted to B99 configuration. Model B99 is illustrated.▼

MODEL C99 AIRLINER

The Model C99 first flight occurred on June 20, 1980 with Beech engineering test pilot Jim Dolbee at the helm. The C99 incorporated a redesigned two-bus electrical system featuring solid-state voltage regulation, improved hydraulic landing gear system and a stronger wing spar structure. Powerplants chosen for the C99 were modular-concept UACL PT6A-36, rated at 715 shp for enhanced high

altitude, hot-day performance. Water/methanol injection was optional, the enlarged cargo pod held 600 pounds and maximum takeoff weight was 11,300 pounds. Model C99 was produced at Beech's Selma, Alabama Division. A total of 71 Model C99 were built from 1982 to 1986. Model C99 illustrated is U-50, a Model 99 rebuilt by Beech in 1980 as the C99 prototype.

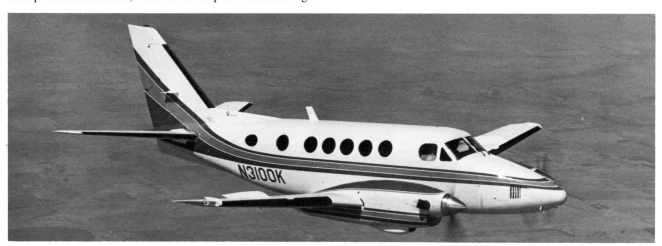

MODEL 100/A100 KING AIR

Unveiled in May, 1969, the Model 100 ascended the throne as Beech Aircraft Corporation's largest King Air. Designed to accomodate executives in luxury or 13 passengers in commuter airline dress, the Model 100 featured wings, tail and powerplants from the Model 99 married to a fuselage of the same cross-section as the Model 90 King Air but longer in length. First flown on March 17, 1969, the Model 100 mounted two PT6A-28 engines rated at 680 shp for takeoff and 620 shp for cruise, giving the flagship a maximum cruise speed of 287 mph. Gross weight was 10,600 pounds...the highest for any corporate King Air at that time. Fuel capacity was 388 gallons with auxiliary tanks holding 82 gallons. The Model 100's pressurization system was limited to a maximum differential of 4.7 psid and the same electrically-operated horizontal stabilizer trim

system used in the Model 99 Airliner was installed on the Model 100 series. 89 airplanes were built from 1969 to 1970. In 1971, the Model A100 King Air replaced the Model 100 on the Beechcraft production lines. Basically an advanced version, the A100 featured a 900-pound increase in maximum takeoff gross weight to 11,500 pounds, carried an additional 96 gallons of fuel that stretched range to 1,542 statute miles at an altitude of 21,000 feet. Four-blade propellers with shorter span improved ground clearance during taxi and landing operations. The A100 cruised through the sky at 271 mph at 21,000 feet and could climb to a service ceiling of 24,850 feet. Model A100 first flight: March 20, 1970. A100 production ended in 1979 after 157 were built. Model A100 is illustrated. Note small wing fences installed to control airflow separation over ailerons at high angle of attack/low airspeeds.

◄ U-21F

The U.S. Army purchased five Model A100 King Airs in 1971 to serve as pressurized transports. Designated U-21F, the Beech constructor numbers were c/n B-95 - c/n B-99, Army serial number s/n 70-15908 - 70-15912. All five were produced and delivered in 1971. Engines were PT6A-28, 680 shp. Second production U-21F is illustrated in standard U.S. Army livery.

MODEL B100 KING AIR

Beech Aircraft Corporation engaged a second-source supplier of engines for the very successful Model A100 King Air in 1974 when Garrett AiResearch TPE-331-6-251B/252 fixed shaft turboprop powerplants were certified on the Model A100 creating the B100 King Air. First flight was March 20, 1975. Beech had already flight-tested Garrett's TPE-series on a company-owned King Air in 1972 as a feasability study on a possible new model with Garrett power. Producing 840 shp flat-rated to 715 shp, the TPE-331 gave the B100 a maximum cruising speed of 306 mph, with a cabin altitude of 8,000 feet at 21,200 feet. Range was 1,501 statute miles. The B100 was produced until 1983. 137 were built.

MODEL 200 SUPER KING AIR

After four years of research and development, Beech introduced the Model 200 Super King Air in 1973. Known as the Model 101 in 1969, the designation became Model 200 and wind tunnel testing of the airplane's most salient feature, a large T-tail, consumed 375 hours. The distinctive T-empennage raised the tail up out of the wing's downwash, allowing the stabilizer and elevator to operate in relatively smooth, undisturbed air. Development accelerated in 1970 and two prototypes (BB-1/BB-2) were constructed, the first flying on October 27, 1972 and the second December 15, 1972. Beech test pilot Bud Francis was in command for both inaugural flights. The Super King Air was powered by two Pratt & Whitney UACL PT6A-41 turboprop engines rated at 850 shp each, and could deliver that power up to 106 degrees F. 544 gallons of fuel were carried in wing/nacelle tanks and two auxiliary tanks located in the wing centersection that was two feet wider than the A100's. Wingspan increased to 54 feet six inches, length 43 feet nine inches

and T-tail height 14 feet 11 1/2 inches. With extra power and wingspan, the Model 200's maximum takeoff gross weight was 12,500 pounds, useful load 5,275 pounds and maximum speed 333 mph. Maximum pressurization system differential was increased to 6.0 psid, resulting in a cabin altitude of 6,740 feet at 25,000 feet or a sea level cabin at 13,820 feet. Model 200's cabin seated up to eight in typical King Air surroundings, air conditioning was standard along with complete wing/tail/propeller deice and windshield anti-ice equipment. Tricycle landing gear continued to use tried and proven electro-mechanical system. Certified in December, 1973, initial deliveries of the Super King Air began in February, 1974. The Model 200 proved to be Beech Aircraft Corporation's crowning achievement in the decade of the 1970s, establishing itself as one of the most popular turboprop airplanes in the world. Model 200 illustrated is N200KA, a Beech demonstrator named "The Free Enterprise". Over 830 Model 200's were built from 1974 to 1981.

MODEL B200 SUPER KING AIR

In 1981, the Model B200 Super King Air took over as Beech's top-of-the-line turboprop. Equipped with (UACL) PT6A-42 engines that retained a rating of 850 shp but incorporated improved hot section components that enabled better climb and high altitude performance, cruise speed increased to 312 mph, pressurization differential increased to 6.5 psid and zero fuel weight (maximum weight of airplane with no fuel) was 11,000 pounds. A double-wide cockpit pedestal made flight deck entry/egress easier and many minor improvements were made to the interior. Next major changes to the Super King Air occurred in 1984, when a 3,000 psi hydraulic landing gear system replaced the electro-mechanical installation effective c/n BB-1193 and after; McCauley propellers were installed effective c/n BB-1193. Price (1987): $2,325,750.

Model 200 instrument panel illustrates a typically-equipped Super King Air, with digital display avionics, color weather radar and complete autopilot/flight director.

MODEL 200T SUPER KING AIR

In 1976, Beech modified Model 200 Super King Air c/n BB-186 into c/n BT-1, a company demonstrator equipped with 50-gallon wing tip tanks for increased endurance and range. Designed for maritime patrol, special large, bulged observation windows were installed in the aft cabin section, surveillance radar was housed under the fuselage and a lower fuselage fairing accomodated various photographic equipment for reconnaissance purposes. Electronic control and monitoring consoles were installed in the cabin. Able to remain on station for more than eight hours (at recommended power settings), Model 200T was another example of the Beechcraft Super King Air's inherent versatility. A 3,000 psi hydraulic landing gear system became standard effective c/n BT-31 and after, replacing electro-mechanical installation of constructor number BT-1 -BT-30. Model 200T, N2067D is illustrated. Note camera fairing, visible under fuselage, bulged observation windows and streamlined tip tanks. 31 200T were built from 1976 to 1987. All were 200T originally assigned Model 200 constructor numbers, then reassigned BT constructor numbers. Price (1987): $2,472,500.

PD 290 (EXPERIMENTAL)

In 1975, Beech used the first Model 200 Super King Air, c/n BB-1, as a testbed for aerodynamic/systems investigations using turbofan engines. Two Pratt & Whitney JT-15D-4 powerplants were installed and PD 290 (Preliminary Design 290) flew for the first time on March 12, 1975 with Beech engineering test pilot Bud Francis in the left seat. PD 290 made its last flight on September 30, 1977, after accumulating 93.3 hours during 103 test flights. ▼

◄   MODEL 200 SUPER KING AIR - C-12A

The first Model 200's to enter military service were c/n BB-3, BB-4 and BB-5 that were converted to A100-1 airplanes for the U.S. Army in 1974. That same year, the Army and U.S. Air Force ordered 20 and 14 Super King Airs respectively to be designated C-12A, Beech designation Model A200. Basically off-the-shelf airplanes, 20 were produced in 1975 (10 Army, 10 USAF), followed in 1976 by 32 airplanes (12 Army, 20 USAF) and 18 for the Army in 1977. In 1978, 20 airplanes were accepted by USAF and were the last C-12A produced. U.S. Air Force (foreground) and U.S. Army Model A200/C-12A are illustrated in original livery.

MODEL 200/B200 SUPER KING AIR - UC-12 SERIES

The U.S. Navy purchased nine Model A200C in 1979 designated UC-12B, c/n BJ-1 -BJ-9, for use as personnel and utility transports for both the Navy and the U.S. Marine Corps. Basically off-the-shelf airplanes, all were equipped with the 52-inch by 52-inch, upward-opening cargo door of the commercial Model 200C. 27 additional airplanes were ordered in 1980, c/n BJ-10 -BJ-36 and another 22 in 1981 and 8 in 1982. A total of 66 UC-12B were produced from 1979 to 1982. UC-12Bs illustrated in formation flight, with U.S. Marine aircraft in background.

MODEL 300 SUPER KING AIR

The Model 300 Super King Air was certified under Special Federal Aviation Regulation 41C, that permitted small, propeller-driven airplanes to exceed 12,500 pounds maximum gross weight if additional airworthiness standards were met. Beech used a Model 200 Super King Air, c/n BB-343, to develop the 300's systems and the first flight as a Model 300 testbed (with PT6A-60A engines) occurred on October 6, 1981 with pilots Bud Francis and George Bromley aboard. BB-343 proved out the added airworthiness requirements called out in SFAR 41C. These included: more comprehensive fatigue testing of critical airframe structures such as wings, spars and empennage; increased fire containment for engine cowlings; improved fire detection and extinguishing capabilities, emergency exit on each side of the cabin if less than 15 seats are installed; improved fire resistant materials for interior and additional crashworthiness requirements for fuel containment after a minor crash landing. United Aircraft of Canada, Ltd (UACL) PT6A-60A turboprop engines rated at 1050 shp, housed in pitot-type, fire-containment cowlings turned four-blade, constant-speed, hydraulically actuated, reversible propellers at 1700 rpm to reduce cabin/cockpit noise level. Fuel capacity: 539 gallons useable. Maximum takeoff gross weight: 14,000 pounds, zero fuel weight: 11,500 pounds. Maximum operating speed: 259 KIAS (.58 Mach). The tricycle landing gear is operated by a 3,000 psi system. 27 Model 300 were produced in 1984, 60 in 1985 and 23 in 1986. Model 300 first flight: September 3, 1983, c/n FA-1 flown by Beech engineering test pilot Vaughn Gregg. Price (1987): $2,659,650.

MODEL 38P LIGHTNING - TPE-331-9 (EXPERIMENTAL)

Intended strictly for use as a flying proof-of-concept aircraft to investigate the feasability of a pressurized, turboprop Beechcraft, the Model 38P "Lightning" used a modified Model 58P Baron pressurized fuselage mounted between engine-less wings. The only prototype built, c/n EJ-1, was fitted with a Garrett AiResearch TPE-331-9 rated at 550 shp initially, increased to 630 shp during

the flight test program. 38P made its first flight on June 14, 1982 with Beech engineering test pilot Lou Johansen at the controls. A total of 133 flights over a period of 100.7 hours yielded valuable information about the compatability of turboprop engine with the Model 58P airframe. Last flight of the Garrett-powered Lightning was November 14, 1983.

◄MODEL 38P LIGHTNING - PT6A-40 (EXPERIMENTAL)

The PD336 Lightning prototype, c/n EJ-1, was also fitted with a UACL PT6A-40 powerplant flat-rated to 630 shp swinging the same 92-inch diameter, three-blade, reversible propeller used on the earlier Garrett-powered ship. Intended to evaluate performance of the 58P airframe with a Pratt & Whitney powerplant, first flight was March 9, 1984, flown by Lou Johansen. Beech cancelled the Lightning program soon after the March first flight, but engineering flight tests continued in accordance with Federal Aviation Regulations Part 23 to collect as much certification-related information as possible. A total of 68 flights were made over a period of 55.7 hours. Last flight of the 5,800-pound maximum takeoff weight Model 38P was August 8, 1984.

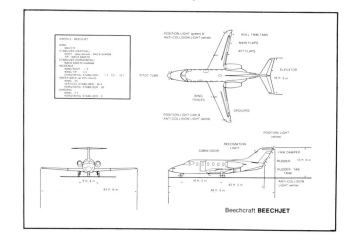

MODEL 400 BEECHJET

Mitsubishi's successful Diamond-series executive aircraft product line was purchased by Beech Aircraft Corporation in 1986. Renamed "Beechjet" and assigned the designation Model 400, the seven passenger plus crew of two jet featured a new Beechcraft-designed interior, 732 gallons of fuel carried in two integral (wet cell) wing tanks and two aft fuselage tanks. A pressurization differential of 9.0 psid provided sea level comfort up to 24,000 feet, and a

6,400-foot cabin at 41,000 feet. Wingspan: 43.5 feet; length: 48.4 feet; height: 13.8 feet. Range with IFR fuel reserves: 1,530 nautical miles. Powered by two Pratt & Whitney JT-15D-5 engines producing 2,900 pounds thrust, the Beechjet has a maximum speed at 29,000 feet of 530 mph (461 knots) and can be fitted with optional Rohr thrust reversers. Maximum takeoff weight: 15,780 pounds. Eight Model 400 were produced in 1986. First 1987 Beechjet was c/n RJ-17. Price (1987): $3,270,000.

MODEL 1900/1900C AIRLINER

Acting in the wake of airline deregulation, Beech Aircraft Corporation designed the Model 1900 Airliner to meet the requirements of regional and commuter airlines who were experiencing rapid growth during 1978-1982. Starting with a basic Model 200 Super King Air cockpit, nose section, empennage and wings, Beech engineers designed a completely new main spar without bolts, making the wing essentially one unit from tip to tip. The cabin section was much longer than that of a Model 200 or 300 Super King Air and seated up to 19 passengers in pressurized comfort. Taking advantage of advanced aerodynamic concepts, Beech installed fixed, wing-like appendages called "stabilons" on the aft fuselage to provide the increased longitudinal stability required over the 1900's wide CG range. Smaller "tailets" were installed on the undersurface of the horizontal stabilizer to provide increased directional stability. The original design included two airstair doors; one at the front and one at the rear, and were designated as UA-series. Engines: two UCAL PT6A-65B turboprop engines, each flat-rated to 1,100 shp. Four-blade, composite propellers decreased overall weight and maintenance. Fuel capacity: 425 gallons in wing and centerwing tanks. Maximum takeoff weight: 16,600 pounds. A 3,000 psi hydraulic landing gear system was installed along with a single ACM (air cycle machine) to provide environmental comfort. Model 1900 first flight: September 3, 1982, c/n UA-1, flown by Beech engineering test pilot Eric Griffin and flight test engineer Bryan Mee. Model 1900 is illustrated. Note two airstair doors. Only three UA-series were produced: c/n UA-1 - UA-3, with UA-1 serving as the Model 1900 prototype.

MODEL 1900C/1900C-1 AIRLINER/EXEC-LINER

Designated as UB-series airplanes, the Beechcraft Model 1900C featured a 52-inch by 52-inch cargo door in the left, aft fuselage section that provided easy loading and unloading of baggage and cargo. The majority of 1900's in service are Model 1900C, including several airplanes configured for corporate use known as "King Air Exec-Liner". A total of 66 1900C were produced from 1984 to 1986. An advanced version, designated the 1900C-1 UC-series with completely redesigned fuel system featuring a wet wing, entered production in 1987 beginning with c/n UC-1. Holding up to 670 gallons of useable fuel, range increased to 1,533 nautical miles from the 1900's 794 nautical mile range. Engines: two UACL PT6A-65B flat-rated to 1,100 shp each. Nine U.S. regional airlines were operating the Model 1900C in 1987. Egypt ordered advanced, special mission Model 1900C-1 aircraft in 1986, with deliveries beginning in 1988. The U.S. Army procured six 1900C-1 for the Air National Guard, designated C-12J for use as transports with first deliveries in 1987. Model 1900C-1 price (1987): $3,691,500. 1900C illustrated.

MODEL 2000 STARSHIP 1

First flown as an 85% scale proof-of-concept vehicle in 1983, the Model 2000 Starship 1 was designed as the foundation for Beech's next generation aircraft. The Model 2000's basic design was developed using advanced computer-aided techniques, including its tandem-wing configuration. Both the aft, main wing and the smaller, variable-geometry forward wing generate lift, with pitch control through elevators mounted on the forward wing. Large, four-segment Fowler-type flaps mounted on the wing's trailing edge extend when the forward wing sweeps forward to provide extra lift for landing, retract after takeoff when the forward wing sweeps aft to cruise position. Starship 1 airframe is constructed primarily of advanced composites such as graphite and epoxy instead of traditional aluminum alloys. Vertical tipsails at end of each wing provide directional stability and mount small rudders for yaw control. Aft-mounted location of UACL PT6A-67 engines reduce cabin noise and vibration levels, minimize thrust asymmetry under single-engine conditions. Three prototypes were performing extensive certification testing by June, 1987. Model 2000 illustrated are c/n NC-1 and NC-2, the first and second full-size prototypes.

Starship 1 flight deck featured CRT screens for primary flight information such as airplane attitude, heading and navigation. Powerplant system status is monitored by microprocessors, with N1 speed, ITT (interstage turbine temperature) torque, propeller rpm and oil pressure/temperature displayed on screen. Primary airframe system annunciators are located in glareshield. Pedestal controls and subpanels are similar to King Air series.

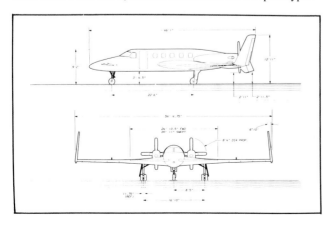

MODEL 2000 STARSHIP 1 - NC-2

Starship 1 main wing spans 54.39 feet, fuselage length 46.08 feet and height to the top of each tipsail 13 feet. Maximum speed of 405 mph (352 knots) was achieved by careful aerodynamic control of boundary layer flow across wing surfaces to minimize drag. With forward wing in landing position and flaps fully extended, Starship 1 landed at relatively slow speed and could stop in very short distances with application of full reverse thrust from its 1,200 shp turboprop powerplants. The first full-size Starship 1, c/n NC-1, was assigned to complete stability and control testing for Federal

Aviation Administration (FAA) certification and first flew February 15, 1986 with pilot Bud Francis and flight test engineer Tom Carr on board. NC-1 also received various aerodynamic modifications to enhance performance, including specially-designed aluminum propellers and highly tapered propeller spinners. Roll control was accomplished by conventional elevons located on outboard main wing trailing edge. The second prototype Starship 1, c/n NC-2 (N3042S) served as a flying testbed for the airplane's 3,000 psi hydraulic landing gear system, multi-bus electrical system, fully automatic, electronically-controlled pressurization system and the environmental system. NC-2 was fully instrumented to record data on systems performance for engineering review. N3042S was also employed to perform initial water ingestion tests for the PT6A-67 engines and icing tests for certification. Starship 1 featured a liquid freezing level depressant (TKS-type) main wing/forward wing anti-icing system. N3042S, c/n NC-2 is illustrated with forward wing swept back to cruise position. First flight was June 14, 1986 with pilot Lou Johansen and flight test engineer Tom Schaffstall on the flight deck.

MODEL 2000 STARSHIP 1 - NC-3

The third prototype Starship 1 joined the flight test program after making its first flight on January 5, 1987 piloted by Tom Carr and flight test engineer Tony Marlow. N3234S, c/n NC-3, was the first Starship 1 designed for a maximum takeoff weight of 14,000 pounds…1,500 pounds more than NC-1 and NC-2's gross weight of 12,500 pounds. Structural and damage tolerance testing of the Model 2000 concentrated primarily on the main and forward wing test specimens that were cycled-tested to simulate 20,000 hours aloft, then both wings were intentionally damaged at critical points and cycle-tested again for another 20,000 hours. Starship 1's fuselage was subjected to a similar series of tests to ensure airworthiness at the 14,000-pound maximum takeoff weight. Model 2000 useful load: 5,286 pounds; zero fuel weight: 11,800 pounds with a two-engine rate of climb exceeding 3,000 feet per minute. Starship 1, c/n NC-3 is illustrated. Note five-blade propellers, metal leading edge for anti-ice fluid weepage, small wing fences adjacent to elevons. Model 2000 price (1987): $3,677,587.

In 1955 Beech obtained exclusive rights to license-build the Morane-Saulnier MS 760 "Paris Jet". Seating four in pressurized cabin, 410 mph twin-engine jet was too early for American market.

Supersonic AQM-37C can be air launched to fly from 1,000 feet to 80,000 feet, simulating up to Mach 3 speed of incoming enemy aircraft or cruise missiles. Rocket-powered, the AQM-37C is capable of performing realistic combat maneuvers, allowing tactical fighters to experience authentic engagement scenarios.

BQM-126A subsonic target drone can carry 100 pounds internally or 220 pounds externally, uses a digital autopilot and remote control command. The U.S. Navy uses the BQM-126A to simulate aircraft and cruise missile threats against a variety of targets, such as ships, aircraft and land-based facilities. Reuseable drone has a single Microturbo North American TRI 60-2/097 engine, can perform 7G turns and fly from sea level up to 40,000 feet.

APPENDIX A

BEECHCRAFT APPROVED TYPE CERTIFICATES

MODEL	APPROVED TYPE CERTIFICATE	DATE
Model 17 Series		
17R	496	12-20-32
A17F	548	8-08-34
A17FS	577	7-06-35
B17L	560	12-04-34
B17B	560	4-29-36
SB17L	560	11-01-35
B17E	566	5-09-35
B17R	579	7-22-35
C17L	602	4-16-36
C17B	602	4-16-36
SC17L	602	4-16-36
SC17B	602	4-16-36
C17E	615	8-13-36
C17R	604	5-06-36
SC17R	604	11-07-39
D17A	713	5-02-37
D17B	638	9-08-41
D17R	638	5-20-37
D17S	649	7-16-37
SD17S	649	9-08-41
E17L	641	9-01-37
E17B	641	9-08-41
SE17B	641	8-26-38
F17D	689	8-26-38
SF17D	689	6-10-41
G17S	779	10-11-46

NOTE: Military derivatives of Model 17 series:

Model B17R - UC-43H
Model C17B - UC-43G
Model C17L - UC-43J
Model C17R - JB-1, UC-43E
Model D17A - UC-43F
Model D17B - UC-43A
Model D17S - UC-43, UC-43B, GB-1, GB-2
Model D17W - UC-43K
Model E17B - UC-43D
Model F17D - UC-43C

MODEL	APPROVED TYPE CERTIFICATE	DATE
Model 18 Series		
18A	TC 630	3-04-37
S18A	TC 630	10-13-41
18B	TC 656	10-29-37
S18B	TC 656	10-29-37
18D	A 684	6-15-38
S18D	A 684	6-15-38
A18A	A 684	5-07-40
SA18A	A 684	5-07-40
A18D	A 684	5-07-40
SA18D	A 684	5-07-40
18S	A 710	11-2-39
B18S	A 710	4-17-40
C18S	A 757	9-23-44
D18CT	A 770	6-3-47
D18S	A 765	4-26-46
D18C	A 765	7-16-47
E18S	A 765	7-19-54
E18S-9700	A 765	1-19-59
G18S	A 765	10-08-59
H18	A 765	7-11-62

MILITARY DERIVATIVES OF COMMERCIAL MODEL 18 SERIES

C-45G, TC-45G, C-45H, TC-45H, TC-45J, UC-45J,	A 765	3-03-58

MODEL	APPROVED TYPE CERTIFICATE	DATE
SNB-5	A 765	5-10-62
RC-45J, SNB-5P	A 765	1-14-69
JRB-6	A 765	8-30-63
3N, 3NM, 3TM (Canada)	A 765	1-31-68
AT-11, SNB-1	A 2-582	5-02-46

NOTE: Army Air Force AT-11 and Navy SNB-1 were granted Group Two approval #2-582 by Civil Aeronautics Authority on 5-2-46 for licensing as 4PCLM (4 Place Cabin Land Monoplane) with two Pratt & Whitney R-985-SB engines of 450 hp each. All AT-11 and SNB-1 c/n were eligible at 7,835 pound gross weight.

NOTE: The following aircraft were military derivatives of the commercial Model C18S:

C-45, C-45A UC-45B, UC-45F, AT-7, AT-7A, AT-7B, AT-7C, JRB-1, JRB-2, JRB-3, JRB-4, SNB-2, SNB-2C, AT-11	A 757	9-23-44
AT-10	L-12-2	5-14-47

MODEL	APPROVED TYPE CERTIFICATE	DATE
Model 19 - Model 23 - Model 24 Series		
23	A1CE	3-15-60
A23	A1CE	6-07-63
A23A	A1CE	11-05-65
A23-19	A1CE	12-09-65
A23-24	A1CE	3-07-66
A24	A1CE	2-05-70
19A	A1CE	8-31-67
M19A	A1CE	12-09-69
B19	A1CE	2-13-70
B23 (Normal category)	A1CE	12-13-67
B23 (Aerobatic)	A1CE	11-22-68
C23	A1CE	2-13-70
A24R	A1CE	12-23-69
B24R	A1CE	6-18-73
C24R	A1CE	10-01-76

MODEL	APPROVED TYPE CERTIFICATE	DATE
Model 33 - Model 35 Series		
35	A777	3-25-47
A35	A777	7-15-48
B35	A777	12-28-49
C35	A777	1-16-51
35R	A777	6-06-51
D35	A777	1-05-53
E35	A777	1-15-54
F35	A777	1-05-55
G35	A777	12-06-55
H35	3A15	12-01-56
J35	3A15	11-13-57
K35	3A15	10-29-58
M35	3A15	10-02-59
N35	3A15	10-20-61
P35	3A15	10-20-61
S35	3A15	1-03-64
V35	3A15	10-22-65
V35TC	3A15	10-22-65
V35A	3A15	10-22-65
V35A-TC	3A15	10-22-65
V35B	3A15	10-06-69
V35B-TC	3A15	10-06-69
35-33	3A15	11-13-59
35-A33	3A15	11-03-60
35-B33	3A15	10-03-61
35-C33	3A15	12-02-64
35-C33A	3A15	1-20-66

74

MODEL	APPROVED TYPE CERTIFICATE	DATE
C33A	3A15	1-20-66
D33	A-CE	8-04-66

NOTE: Model D33 was experimental ground attack aircraft issued a Provisonal Type Certificate only. No commercial D33 were built.

MODEL	APPROVED TYPE CERTIFICATE	DATE
E33	3A15	10-10-67
E33A	3A15	10-10-67
E33C	3A15	9-09-68
F33	3A15	10-24-69
F33A	3A15	10-24-69
F33C	3A15	10-24-69
G33	3A15	3-17-71

Model 45 and T-34C Series

A5 (YT-34 prototype)	5A3	7-17-50
A45 (T-34A)	5A3	9-21-53
B45 (T-34 export version)	5A3	9-21-53
D45 (T-34B)	5A3	3-09-60
T-34C	A26CE	8-25-78
T-34C-1	A26CE	12-17-76

Model 36 Series

36	3A15	5-01-68
A36	3A15	10-24-69
A36TC	3A15	12-07-78
B36TC	3A15	1-15-82

Model 50 Series

50	5A4	5-25-51
B50	5A4	7-31-53
C50	5A4	10-13-54
D50	5A4	12-06-55
E50	5A4	12-01-56
D50A	5A4	10-29-57
D50C	5A4	11-13-59
D50E	5A4	11-10-60
D50E (5990 pound MTOW)	5A4	3-21-74
F50	5A4	10-29-57
D50B	5A4	11-10-58
G50	5A4	11-10-58
H50	5A4	11-13-59
N50	5A4	11-13-59
J50	5A4	11-16-60

Model 95-55 And Model 55 Series

95-B55	3A16	9-09-63
95-B55A	3A16	10-31-68
95-B55B	3A16	8-26-64
95-C55	3A16	8-18-65
95-C55A	3A16	10-31-68
D55	3A16	10-17-67
E55	3A16	11-12-69
E55A	3A16	6-16-70

Model 56 Series

56TC	3A16	5-19-67
A56TC	3A16	11-12-69

Model 58 Series

58	3A16	11-19-69
58A	3A16	11-10-70
58P	A23CE	5-21-74
58PA	A23CE	5-12-76
58TC	A23CE	1-23-76
58TCA	A23CE	5-12-76

Model 60 Series

MODEL	APPROVED TYPE CERTIFICATE	DATE
60	A12CE	2-01-68
A60	A12CE	1-30-70
B60	A12CE	10-05-73

Model 65 Series

65	3A20	2-04-59
65-80	3A20	2-20-62
65-A80	3A20	3-26-64
65-A80 (8800 pound MTOW)	3A20	10-22-65
65-B80	3A20	10-22-65
65-88	3A20	9-21-65
65-90	3A20	5-19-64
65-A90	3A20	3-07-66
A65	3A20	11-03-66
A65 (8200 pound MTOW)	3A20	10-09-67
65-A90-1	3A20	4-27-66
65-A90-2	3A20	3-20-69
65-A90-3	3A20	3-20-69
65-A90-4	3A20	12-10-71
70	3A20	11-27-68
B90	3A20	11-14-67
C90	3A20	10-23-70
C90-1	3A20	10-23-70
C90A	3A20	12-1-83
E90	3A20	4-13-72
F90	A31CE	5-18-79
F90-1	A31CE	5-18-79
H90	3A20	3-23-77

Model 76

76	A29CE	1-24-78

Model 77

77	A30CE	4-15-80

Model 95 Series

95	3A16	6-18-57
B95	3A16	11-13-59
B95A	3A16	3-09-61
D95A	3A16	5-17-63
D95A	3A16	10-31-68
E95	3A16	10-17-67

Model 99 Series

99	A14CE	5-02-68
99A	A14CE	2-10-69
99A	A14CE	6-10-70
A99	A14CE	2-19-71
A99A	A14CE	2-19-71
B99	A14CE	3-27-72
C99	A14CE	7-27-81

Model 100 Series

100	A14CE	7-24-69
A100	A14CE	5-07-71
A100A	A14CE	11-01-72
A100C	A14CE	12-14-73
B100	A14CE	12-01-75

Model 200 Series

200	A24CE	12-14-73
200C	A24CE	2-21-79
200T	A24CE	12-15-76
200CT	A24CE	2-21-79
A200	A24CE	6-20-75

MODEL	APPROVED TYPE CERTIFICATE	DATE
A200C	A24CE	2-21-79
A200CT	A24CE	4-17-80
B200	A24CE	2-13-81
B200C	A24CE	2-13-81
B200T	A24CE	2-13-81
B200CT	A24CE	2-13-81
Model 300		
300	A24CE	1-24-84
Model 400		
400	A16SW	5-1-86

NOTE: Mitsubishi Model MU-300-10 was originally certified under ATC A14SW. When Beech Aircraft Corporation obtained the MU-300-10 it received ATC A16SW that incorporates certification for the MU-300-10 and the Model 400 Beechjet. Beechcraft Service Bulletin 2140 permits owners of Mitsubishi airplanes to retrofit their jets to Model 400 configuration.

Model 1900

1900	A24CE	11-22-83

APPENDIX B

The following compilation details commercial Beechcraft production from 1932 through 1987. Four major segments are presented: model, year produced, constructor number (serial number) and total airplanes built during each model year. Information is presented in numerical order by model.

Additional information regarding military production of certain Beechcraft models is included with the commercial production list. Beech constructor numbers were issued consecutively (regardless of model or type) from 1932 until 1945, when each model was given a discrete identity code.

The Model 17 series listing presents total airplanes produced per calendar year and constructor numbers only where information is known to be accurate and verifiable. Model 18 listing indicates total aircraft delivered per year, not total produced. Information for this listing was procured from official Beech Aircraft Corporation files.

COMMERCIAL PRODUCTION/DELIVERIES - 1932-1942

MODEL	YEAR	CONSTRUCTOR NUMBER	TOTAL DELIVERED
17R	1932	1	0
17R	1933	1	1
17R	1934	2	1
A17F	1934	5	1
A17FS	1934	11	1
B17B	1934	20	1
B17E	1935	22, 49, 51	3
B17L	1934	3, 4, 6-10, 12-21	16
B17L	1935	23-49	26
B17L	1936	58-61	4
B17R	1935	38, 50, 52-56	7
B17R	1936	63-66, 68-72	9
C17L	1936	83, 84, 100, 105, 107, 109	6
C17L	1937	124	1
C17R	1936	73-77, 79-82, 113, 114	11
C17R	1937	115, 116, 118-120, 122	6
SC17R	1936	113	1
C17B	1936	67, 84-99, 101-104, 106, 108, 110-112	25
C17B	1937	121, 123, 125-135	13
SC17B	1936	99	1
C17E	1936	78	1
C17E	1937	117	1

MODEL	YEAR	CONSTRUCTOR NUMBER	TOTAL DELIVERED

NOTE: C17E c/n 78/117 sold to Tokyo Hikoki Seisaku-Jo in Japan and assembled there under supervision of Beechcrafter Virgil H. Adamson in 1937. Aviation historian Richard M. Bueschel states that 20 C17E were built by the Japanese firm under license from Beech Aircraft Company between 1937-1940.

E17B	1937	138-145, 149-160, 162, 163, 189-196	30
E17B	1938	197, 198, 204-210, 212, 213, 219, 227, 228, 231-234, 251	19
E17B	1939	274, 280, 336	3
E17B	1940	388	1
SE17B	1937	160	1
SE17B	1938	210, 227	2
SE17B	1939	280	1
E17L	1937	161	1
F17D	1938	211, 225, 226, 229, 240-250, 252, 255	18
F17D	1939	256-262, 270-273, 275-277, 281-283, 307-312, 330-335, 337-339	32
F17D	1940	389-394, 410	7
F17D	1941	412	1
SF17D	1941	414	1
F17D	1942	413	1
D17A	1939	305, 356-361, 363	8
D17A	1940	Not Produced	0
D17R	1937	137, 148, 166, 167, 180-182, 184, 188	9
D17R	1938	214, 215, 217, 218, 235-237, 253	8
D17R	1939	278, 289, 313, 325, 326, 328, 329	7
D17R	1940	397, 405	2
D17S	1937	147, 165, 168, 179, 183, 185-187	8
D17S	1938	199-203, 216, 217, 238, 239, 254	10
D17S	1939	263, 264, 279, 284-288, 295-304, 306, 314, 327, 354, 355, 362	24
SD17S	1939	279	1
D17S	1940	385-387, 395, 396, 398-404, 406-408	16
D17S	1941	415-424	10
D17S	1942	Not Produced	0
D17W	1937	164	1

NOTE: Two D17W were built, but only c/n 164 was delivered as a D17W. The first D17W was c/n 136, built in February, 1937. Reengined before delivery with Wright R-975 of 420 hp as D17R.

18A	1937	62	1
18A	1940	291	1
S18A	1937	172	1
18B	1937	170, 171	2
18B	1938	174	1
S18B	1937	173	1
18D	1938	175, 176, 169, 220	4
18D	1939	221, 223, 224, 265, 267, 268	6
S18D	1938	177, 178	2
18S	1939	266, 269, 294	3
18S	1940	292, 316, 430, 431, 433, 434	6
18R	1940	321, 376-380	6
C18S	1940	432	1
C18S	1941	445	1
A18A	1940	290	1

NOTE: By late 1941 when commercial production ceased because of the war effort, Beech had produced approximately 383 airplanes, comprised of 270 Model 17 series and 113 Model 18 series. Of the Model 17 series, 61 F17D were built, followed by 69 D17S, 57 E17B, 44 B17L and 39 C17B. The majority of military Model 18 produced were C-45 and F-2 versions of the Model C18S and B18S respectively.

BEECHCRAFT COMMERCIAL PRODUCTION - 1945 - 1987

Model 18 Series

D18S	1945	A-1 - A-37	37
D18S	1946	A-38 - A-333	296
D18S	1947	A-334 - A-408	75
D18S	1948	A-409 - A-476	68
D18S	1949	A-477 - A-519	43
D18S	1950	A-520 - A-551	32

76

MODEL	YEAR	CONSTRUCTOR NUMBER	TOTAL DELIVERED
D18S	1951	A-552 - A-673	122
D18S	1952	A-674 - A-864	191
D18S	1953	A-865 - A-995	131
D18S	1954	A-996 - A-1019	24
D18S	1956	A-1020 - A-1028	9
D18S	1957	A-1029 - A-1035	7

Model Super E18S Series

MODEL	YEAR	CONSTRUCTOR NUMBER	TOTAL DELIVERED
E18S	1955	BA-1 - BA-112	112
E18S	1956	BA-113 - BA-226	114
E18S	1957	BA-227 - BA-327	101
E18S	1958	BA-328 - BA-402	75
E18S*	1959	BA-403 - BA-433, BA-435 - BA-460	57

*NOTE: 1959 E18S c/n with 9,700-pound gross weight.

E18S	1960	BA-497	1

Model Super G18S Series

MODEL	YEAR	CONSTRUCTOR NUMBER	TOTAL DELIVERED
G18S	1960	BA-434, BA-461 - BA-496, BA-498 - BA-551	91
G18S	1961	BA-552 - BA-562, BA-564 - BA-579, BA-581 - BA-597	44
G18S*	1961	BA-563	1

*NOTE: BA-563 had 9,150-pound gross weight.

G18S	1962	BA-598 - BA-617	20

Model Super H18 Series

MODEL	YEAR	CONSTRUCTOR NUMBER	TOTAL DELIVERED
H18	1963	BA-580, BA-618 - BA-650	34
H18	1964	BA-651 - BA-711	61
H18	1965	BA-712 - BA-734	23
H18	1966	BA-735 - BA-742	8
H18	1967	BA-743 - BA-752	10
H18	1968	BA-753 - BA-755	3
H18	1969	BA-756 - BA-762	7
H18	1970	BA-763 - BA-765	3

Model 19 - Model 23 - Model 24 Series

MODEL	YEAR	CONSTRUCTOR NUMBER	TOTAL DELIVERED
23	1963	M-1, M-2, M-4 - M-554	553

NOTE: These aircraft designated "Musketeer".

A23	1965	M-3, M-555 - M-900	346

NOTE: These aircraft designated "Musketeer II".

MODEL	YEAR	CONSTRUCTOR NUMBER	TOTAL DELIVERED
A23A	1966	M-901 - M-994	94
A23A	1967	M-995 - M-1068	74
A23A	1968	M-1069 - M-1094	26
B23	1968	M-1095 - M-1162	68
B23	1969	M-1163 - M-1284	122
C23	1970	M-1285 - M-1290, M-1292 - M-1297, M-1292 - M-1297, M-1299, M-1300, M-1303	15
C23	1971	M-1291, M-1298, M-1301, M-1302, M-1304 - M-1361	62

NOTE: A23A/B23/C23 series designated "Musketeer Custom III".

MODEL	YEAR	CONSTRUCTOR NUMBER	TOTAL DELIVERED
C23	1972	M-1362 - M-1412, M-1415, M-1419 - M-1423, M-1439, M-1447	56
C23	1973	M-1413, M-1414, M-1416- M-1418, M-1420 - M-1422, M-1424 - M-1438, M-1440 - M-1446, M-1448 - M-1490	73
C23	1974	M-1491 - M-1585, M-1587 - M-1599	108
C23	1975	M-1586, M-1600 - M-1726, M-1728 - M-1747	148
C23	1976	M-1727, M-1748 - M-1874, M-1876 - M-1879	132
C23	1977	M-1875, M-1880 - M-1970, M-1972 - M-1979	100
C23	1978	M-1971, M-1980 - M-2085, M-2087 - M-2092	113
C23	1979	M-2086, M-2093 - M-2223, M-2225 - M-2233	141
C23	1980	M-2224, M-2234 - M-2292	60

MODEL	YEAR	CONSTRUCTOR NUMBER	TOTAL DELIVERED
C23	1981	M-2293 - M-2341	49
C23	1982	M-2342 - M-2368	26
C23	1983	M-2369 - M-2392	24

NOTE: Model C23 from 1972 - 1983 designated "Sundowner 180".

MODEL	YEAR	CONSTRUCTOR NUMBER	TOTAL DELIVERED
A23-19	1966	MB-1 - MB-166	166
A23-19	1967	MB-167 - MB-288	122
19A	1968	MB-289 - MB-392	104
19A	1969	MB-393 - MB-460	68
M19A	1969	MB-461 - MB-480	20
B19	1970	MB-481 - MB-493	13
B19	1971	MB-494 - MB-520	27
B19	1972	MB-521 - MB-557	37
B19	1973	MB-558 - MB-621	64
B19	1974	MB-622 - MB-715, MB-717 - MB-730 *	107

*NOTE: c/n MB-723 not built; replaced by c/n MB-623.

MODEL	YEAR	CONSTRUCTOR NUMBER	TOTAL DELIVERED
B19	1975	MB-716, MB-731 - MB-778	49
B19	1976	MB-779 - MB-813, MB-815, MB-816	37
B19	1977	MB-814, MB-817 - MB-865	50
B19	1978	MB-866 - MB-905	40

NOTE: Model B19 from 1972 - 1978 designated "Sport 150".

MODEL	YEAR	CONSTRUCTOR NUMBER	TOTAL DELIVERED
A23-24	1966	MA-1 - MA-122	122
A23-24	1967	MA-123 - MA-272	150
A23-24	1968	MA-273 - MA-335	63
A23-24	1969	MA-336 - MA-363	28
A24	1970	MA-364 - MA-368	5

NOTE: 1966-1967 A23-24 designated "Musketeer Super".
1968-1969 A23-24 designated "Musketeer Super III".
1970 A24 designated "Musketeer Super". The following list contains c/n for fixed-gear Model A23-24 and A24 that were equipped at the factory with 200 hp Lycoming engines and two-blade, constant-speed propellers. Only 86 airplanes were produced in this configuration:
Model A23-24 - MA-1, MA-85, MA-188, MA-189, MA-190 - MA-192, MA-195 - MA-199, MA-201, MA-210, MA-212, MA-214 - MA-216, MA-219, MA-222, MA-227 - MA-230, MA-236, MA-240, MA-243, MA-246 - MA-248, MA-254, MA-259, MA-260, MA-263, MA-266 - MA-268, MA-280, MA-283, MA-287 - MA-295, MA-297, MA-298, MA-301 - MA-304, MA-306, MA-310 - MA-312, MA-314 - MA-316, MA-318, MA-326, MA-329 - MA-331, MA-334, MA-337, MA-339 - MA-342, MA-344 - MA-346, MA-349, MA-352 - MA-355, MA-357, MA-358, MA-360, MA-362, MA-363.
Model A24: MA-366.

MODEL	YEAR	CONSTRUCTOR NUMBER	TOTAL DELIVERED
A24R	1970	MC-2 - MC-21, MC-24 - MC-38, MC-40, MC-41, MC-44 - MC-47, MC-49 - MC-62, MC-66, MC-67, MC-69, MC-70	59
A24R	1971	MC-22, MC-23, MC-39, MC-42, MC-43, MC-48, MC-63 - MC-65, MC-68, MC-71 - MC-95	35
A24R	1972	MC-96 - MC-150	55
B24R	1973	MC-152 - MC-190	39
B24R	1974	MC-191 - MC-292, MC-294 - MC-304	113
B24R	1975	MC-293, MC-305 - MC-381, MC-383 - MC-385	81
B24R	1976	MC-382, MC-386 - MC-448, MC-450, MC-451	66
C24R	1977	MC-449, MC-452 - MC-532, MC-534 - MC-536	85
C24R	1978	MC-533, MC-537 - MC-619	84
C24R	1979	MC-620 - MC-688, MC-690 - MC-701	81
C24R	1980	MC-689, MC-702 - MC-740	40
C24R	1981	MC-741 - MC-764	24
C24R	1982	MC-765 - MC-782	18
C24R	1983	MC-783 - MC-795	13

NOTE: 1972 - 1983 A24R/B24R/C24R designated "Sierra 200".

Model 25	1940	U.S. Army Air Force	1

Original prototype Model 25 destroyed on May 5, 1941. Not rebuilt.

MODEL	YEAR	CONSTRUCTOR NUMBER	TOTAL DELIVERED
Model 26	1941	U.S. Army Air Force	1,771

Followup design of Model 25. Designated AT-10. Military production only.

MODEL	YEAR	CONSTRUCTOR NUMBER	TOTAL DELIVERED
Model 28	1945	U.S. Army Air Force	2

NOTE: Model 28 became military XA-38 "Grizzly" ground attack aircraft. Only two were built, both experimental prototypes.

Model 33 Series

MODEL	YEAR	CONSTRUCTOR NUMBER	TOTAL DELIVERED
35-33	1960	CD-1 - CD-224, CD-233, CD-234, CD-236, CD-241, CD-246 - CD-250	233
35-A33	1961	CD-225 - CD-232, CD-235, CD-237 - CD-240, CD-242, CD-245, CD-251 - CD-387	154
35-B33	1962	CD-388 - CD-587	200
35-B33	1963	CD-588 - CD-724	137
35-B33	1964	CD-725 - CD-811	87
35-B33	1965	CD-812, CD-813	2
35-C33	1965	CD-814 - CD-970	157
35-C33	1966	CD-971 - CD-981, CD-983 - CD-1056	85
35-C33	1967	CD-1057 - CD-1118	62
35-C33A	1966	CE-1 - CE-102	102
35-C33A	1967	CE-103 - CE-179	77
E33	1968	CD-1119 - CD-1199	81
E33	1969	CD-1200 - CD-1234	35
F33	1970	CD-1235 - CD-1254	20
G33	1972	CD-1255 - CD-1299	45
G33	1973	CD-1300 - CD-1304	5

NOTE: CD-1305 - CD-1325 changed to F33C at factory.

MODEL	YEAR	CONSTRUCTOR NUMBER	TOTAL DELIVERED
E33A	1968	CE-180 - CE-235	56

NOTE: CE-236 - CE-248 changed to E33C at factory.

MODEL	YEAR	CONSTRUCTOR NUMBER	TOTAL DELIVERED
E33A	1969	CE-249, CE-250, CE-260, CE-264 - CE-268, CE-270 - CE-289	29

NOTE: CE-251 - CE-255, CE-257 - CE-259, CE-261 - CE-263, CE-269 changed to E33C at factory. The following G33 and E33A c/n were changed to E33C and F33C at the factory. Old c/n shown in parentheses. From c/n CJ-52 and after no E33A or G33 were converted to F33C configuration.

1968 - E33A to E33C conversion - 13 airplanes:

CJ-1 (CE-236), CJ-2 (CE-237), CJ-3 (CE-238), CJ-4 (CE-239), CJ-5 (CE-240), CJ-6 (CE-241), CJ-7 (CE-242), CJ-8, (CE-243), CJ-9 (CE-244), CJ-10 (CE-245), CJ-11 (CE-246), CJ-12 (CE-247), CJ-13 (CE-248)

1969 - E33A to E33C conversion - 12 airplanes:

CJ-14 (CE-251), CJ-15 (CE-252), CJ-16 (CE-253), CJ-17 (CE-254), CJ-18 (CE-255), CJ-19 (CE-257), CJ-20 (CE-258), CJ-21 (CE-259), CJ-22 (CE-261), CJ-23 (CE-262), CJ-24 (CE-263), CJ-25 (CE-269)

MODEL	YEAR	CONSTRUCTOR NUMBER	TOTAL DELIVERED
F33A	1970	CE-290 - CE-315	26
F33A	1971	CE-316 - CE-349	34
F33A	1972	CE-350 - CE-401	52
F33A	1973	CE-402 - CE-464	63
F33A	1974	CE-465 - CE-535	71
F33A	1975	CE-536 - CE-611	76
F33A	1976	CE-612 - CE-673	62
F33A	1977	CE-674 - CE-743	70
F33A	1978	CE-744 - CE-815	72
F33A	1979	CE-816 - CE-883	68
F33A	1980	CE-884 - CE-928	45
F33A	1981	CE-929 - CE-977	49
F33A	1982	CE-978 - CE-1011	36
F33A	1983	CE-1014 - CE-1023	10
F33A	1984	CE-1024, CE-1025, CE-1027 - CE-1032	8
F33A	1985	CE-1026, CE-1033 - CE-1071,	40
F33A	1986	CE-1072 - CE-1101	29
F33A	1987	CE-1102 - CE-1206	104

MODEL	YEAR	CONSTRUCTOR NUMBER	TOTAL DELIVERED
F33C	1970	CJ-26 - CJ-30	5

NOTE: CJ-26 - CJ-30 standard production F33C.

1973 - G33 to F33C conversion - 9 airplanes:
CJ-31 (CD-1305), CJ-32 (CD-1306), CJ-33 (CD-1307), CJ-34 (CD-1308), CJ-35 (CD-1309), CJ-36 (CD-1310), CJ-37 (CD-1311), CJ-38 (CD-1312), CJ-39 (CD-1313)

1974 - G33 to F33C conversion - 12 airplanes:
CJ-40 (CD-1314), CJ-41 (CD-1315), CJ-42 (CD-1316), CJ-43 (CD-1317), CJ-44 (CD-1318), CJ-45 (CD-1319), CJ-46 (CD-1320), CJ-47 (CD-1321), CJ-48 (CD-1322), CJ-49 (CD-1323), CJ-50 (CD-1324), CJ-51 (CD-1325)

NOTE: CJ-31 - CJ-51 sold to Iran.

MODEL	YEAR	CONSTRUCTOR NUMBER	TOTAL DELIVERED
F33C	1974	CJ-52 - CJ-63	11

NOTE: CJ-52 - CJ-63 standard production F33C.

MODEL	YEAR	CONSTRUCTOR NUMBER	TOTAL DELIVERED
F33C	1975	CJ-64 - CJ-102	39
F33C	1976	CJ-103 - CJ-128	26
F33C	1977	CJ-129	1
F33C	1978	CJ-130 - CJ-148	19
F33C	1979	CJ-149 - CJ-155	7
F33C	1986	CJ-156 - CJ-178*	22

*NOTE: CJ-156 - CJ-176 delivered to Mexican Air Force. CJ-177 and CJ-178 were commercial deliveries.

MODEL	YEAR	CONSTRUCTOR NUMBER	TOTAL DELIVERED
F33C	1987	CJ-179 and after	

Model 35 Series

MODEL	YEAR	CONSTRUCTOR NUMBER	TOTAL DELIVERED
35	1947	D-1 - D-1209	1196*

*NOTE: The following c/n were reworked by Beech in 1951 as a service to owners of Model 35 Bonanzas who desired to update their airplanes. Modifications included structural changes to empennage, wings and fuselage; gross weight increased to 2,650 pounds; remanufactured Continental E-185-11 engine (takeoff power limited to 196 hp). These airplanes received additional improvements found on the Model B35 and C35 Bonanza but retained the Model 35's tubular steel wing center section. The 35R program ended in August, 1951 but some 35R c/n were not completed until 1952. All 13 35R were 1947 Model 35 Bonanzas:

35R - 1947 - 13 airplanes:
R-1 (D-25), R-2 (D-3), R-3 (D-721), R-4 (D-838), R-5 (D-588), R-6 (D-535), R-7 (D-532), R-9 (D-944), R-10 (D-1186), R-11 (D-92), R-12 (D-329), R-13 (D-418)

MODEL	YEAR	CONSTRUCTOR NUMBER	TOTAL DELIVERED
35	1948	D-1210 - D-1500 (except D-1424)	290
35R	1948	R-8 (D-1424)	1
A35	1949	D-1501 - D-2200, D-15001	701

NOTE: D-15001 was a production A35 built strictly for factory experimental work. The high c/n was intentionally chosen because regular production was never expected to reach that number.

MODEL	YEAR	CONSTRUCTOR NUMBER	TOTAL DELIVERED
B35	1950	D-2201 - D-2680	480
C35	1951	D-2681 - D-3090	410
C35	1952	D-3091 - D-3292, D-3294 - D-3400	309
D35	1953	D-3401 - D-3698	298
E35	1954	D-3699 - D-3998, D-3293	301
F35	1955	D-3999 - D-4375, D-4377 - D-4391	392
G35	1956	D-4392 - D-4865, D-4376, D-15002	476

NOTE: D-15002 was a production G35 built strictly for factory experimental work.

MODEL	YEAR	CONSTRUCTOR NUMBER	TOTAL DELIVERED
H35	1957	D-4866 - D-5061, D-5063 - D-5330	464
J35	1958	D-5331 - D-5725, D-5062	396
K35	1959	D-5726 - D-6161	436

MODEL	YEAR	CONSTRUCTOR NUMBER	TOTAL DELIVERED
M35	1960	D-6162 - D-6561	400
N35	1961	D-6562 - D-6841	280
O35	1961	Unknown	1

NOTE: The O35 was an experimental Bonanza equipped with a laminar flow wing and trailing beam-type main landing gear. Entire wing leading edge was a wet cell for increased fuel capacity. Engine was 260 hp IO-470N. No production O35 were built. It is included here strictly because of its alphabetical sequence with other Bonanzas.

MODEL	YEAR	CONSTRUCTOR NUMBER	TOTAL DELIVERED
P35	1962	D-6842 - D-7066	225
P35	1963	D-7067 - D-7139, D-7141 - D-7309	242
S35	1964	D-7310 - D-7639, D-7140	331
S35	1965	D-7640 - D-7967	328
S35	1966	D-7968 - D-7976	9
V35/V3 5TC	1966	D-7977 - D-8301	325

NOTE: The following list contains c/n for 1966 V35TC turbocharged models built concurrently with naturally-aspirated V35 airplanes:
V35TC - 1966 - 37 airplanes:

D-8036, D-8048, D-8057, D-8064, D-8072, D-8075, D-8090, D-8127, D-8133, D-8140, D-8146, D-8153, D-8176, D-8181, S-8184, D-8188, D-8190, D-8194, D-8199, D-8205, D-8210, D-8217, D-8225, D-8229, D-8234, D-8239, D-8242, D-8245, D-8249, D-8255, D-8261, D-8267, D-8274, D-8279, D-8286, D-8294, D-8300

V35	1967	D-8302 - D-8598	297

NOTE: The following list contains c/n for 1967 V35TC turbocharged models built concurrently with naturally-aspirated V35 airplanes:
V35TC - 1967 - 42 airplanes:

D-8307, D-8316, D-8323, D-8328, D-8336, D-8346, D-8353, D-8359, D-8366, D-8373, D-8379, D-8385, D-8393, D-8400, D-8407, D-8419, D-8427, D-8432, D-8438, D-8447, D-8456, D-8465, D-8470, D-8475, D-8481, D-8485, D-8490, D-8496, D-8500, D-8505, D-8509, D-8514, D-8518, D-8526, D-8530, D-8533, D-8540, D-8552, D-8560, D-8567, D-8577, D-8596

V35A/V35A-TC	1968	D-8599 - D-8871	273

NOTE: The following list contains c/n for 1968 V35A-TC turbocharged models built concurrently with naturally-aspirated V35A airplanes:
V35A-TC - 1968 - 26 airplanes:

D-8606, D-8615, D-8625, D-8628, D-8638, D-8652, D-8662, D-8673, D-8681, D-8694, D-8705, D-8715, D-8730, D-8744, D-8763, D-8777, D-8790, D-8810, D-8823, D-8829, D-8835, D-8842, D-8849, D-8855, D-8861, D-8868

V35A/V35A-TC	1969	D-8872 - D-9068	197

NOTE: The following list contains c/n for 1969 V35A-TC turbocharged models built concurrently with naturally-aspirated V35A airplanes:
V35A-TC - 1969 - 20 airplanes:
D-8875, D-8887, D-8901, D-8911, D-8921, D-8930, D-8940, D-8951, D-8961, D-8973, D-8982, D-8992, D-9001, D-9008, D-9019, D-9027, D-9039, D-9048, D-9055, D-9063, D-9070, D-9078, D-9088, D-9107, D-9131, D-9154, D-9180

V35B/V35B-TC	1970	D-9069 - D-9204, D-9207 - D-9211	141

NOTE: The following list contains c/n for 1970 V35B-TC turbocharged models built concurrently with naturally-aspirated V35B airplanes:
V35B-TC - 1970 - 7 airplanes:
D-9070, D-9078, D-9088, D-9107, D-9131, D-9154, D-9180

V35B	1971	D-9205, D-9206, D-9212 - D-9286	77
V35B	1972	D-9287 - D-9390	104
V35B	1973	D-9391 - D-9537	147
V35B	1974	D-9538 - D-9686	149

MODEL	YEAR	CONSTRUCTOR NUMBER	TOTAL DELIVERED
V35B	1975	D-9687 - D-9815	129
V35B	1976	D-9816 - D-9947	132
V35B	1977	D-9948 - D-10068	121
V35B	1978	D-10069 - D-10178	110
V35B	1979	D-10179 - D-10302	124
V35B	1980	D-10303 - D-10353	51
V35B	1981	D-10354 - D-10382	29
V35B	1982	D-10383 - D-10403*	21

*NOTE: D-10403 was last V-tail Bonanza built, delivered to production flight test on 11-2-82. Delivered in May, 1984. Last V-tail Bonanza delivered to a retail customer was D-10399, delivered in August, 1984.

Model 36 Series

MODEL	YEAR	CONSTRUCTOR NUMBER	TOTAL DELIVERED
36	1968	E-1 - E-105	105
36	1969	E-106 - E-184	79
A36	1970	E-185 - E-240	56
A36	1971	E-241 - E-282	42
A36	1972	E-283 - E-363	81
A36	1973	E-364 - E-476	113
A36	1974	E-477 - E-604	128
A36	1975	E-605 - E-765	161
A36	1976	E-766 - E-926	161
A36	1977	E-927 - E-1110, E-1112 - E-1151	224
A36	1978	E-1111, E-1152 - E-1370	224
A36	1979	E-1371 - E-1593	223
A36	1980	E-1594 - E-1765	172
A36	1981	E-1766 - E-1931	166
A36	1982	E-1932 - E-2049	117
A36	1983	E-2050 - E-2103, E-2105 - E-2110	59
A36	1984	E-2104, E-2111 - E-2204	95
A36	1985	E-2205 - E-2277, E-2279 - E-2289, E-2293 - E-2295	87
A36	1986	E-2278, E-2290, E-2291, E-2292, E-2296 - E-2352	60
A36	1987	E-2353 - E-2402	49
A36TC	1979	EA-1 - EA-32	32
A36TC	1980	EA-33 - EA-158	126
A36TC	1981	EA-159 - EA-241, EA-243 - EA-272	113
B36TC	1981	EA-242	1
B36TC	1982	EA-273 - EA-319, EA-321 - EA-323	50
B36TC	1983	EA-324 - EA-388	65
B36TC	1984	EA-320, EA-389 - EA-442	54
B36TC	1985	EA-443 - EA-451	8
B36TC	1986	EA-452 - EA-461	9
B36TC	1987	EA-462 and after	

Model 45 Series

NOTE: Early production Model B45, T-34A and T-34B are listed by deliveries in fiscal year, not calendar year. Beech built commercial and military versions of the Model 45 from 1950 to 1959. Constructor numbers are not presented for these airplanes:

MODEL	YEAR	CONSTRUCTOR NUMBER	TOTAL DELIVERED
A45T	1950	YT-34BH - U.S. Army	3
T-34A	1953-54	U.S. Air Force	88
B45	1953-54	Commercial deliveries	85
T-34A	1954-55	U.S. Air Force	122
T-34B	1954-55	U.S. Navy	45
B45	1954-55	Commercial deliveries	47
T-34A	1955-56	U.S. Air Force	138
T-34B	1955-56	U.S. Navy	219
B45	1955-56	Commercial deliveries	21
T-34B	1956-57	U.S. Navy	147
B45	1956-57	Commercial deliveries	45
T-34B	1957-58	U.S. Navy	12
B45	1957-58	Commercial deliveries	29
B45	1958-59	Commercial deliveries	91

MODEL	YEAR	CONSTRUCTOR NUMBER	TOTAL DELIVERED

NOTE: Fuji Heavy Industries built the T-34A under license for Japan's emerging Self-Defense Force in the 1950s. The Japanese built 137 T-34.

Model 45 Series - Turbine-powered

| 34C | 1979 | GP-1 - GP-6 | 6 |

NOTE: GP-1 - GP-6 originally designated GM-72 - GM-77.

(Refer to 1978 T-34C-1)

Model	Year	Constructor Number	Total Delivered
34C	1984	GP-7 - GP-15	8
34C	1985	GP-16 - GP-50	35
34C	1986	GP-51	1
T-34C	1976	GL-1, GL-2	2
T-34C	1977	GL-3 - GL-72	70
T-34C	1978	GL-73 - GL-138	66
T-34C	1979	GL-139 - GL-163	25
T-34C	1981	GL-164 - GL-184	21
T-34C	1983	GL-232 - GL-237, GL-241, GL-231, GL-238 - GL-240, GL-242 - GL-334	97

NOTE: GL-334 delivered to U.S. Navy 6-84. No T-34C were built in 1985-88.

| T-34C | 1989-90 | GL-335 - GL-353 | 19 |
| T-34C-1 | 1977 | GM-2 - GM-10, GM-14 - GM-20 | 16 |

NOTE: GM-14 built as Beech factory demonstrator.

| T-34C-1 | 1978 | GM-11 - GM-13, GM-21 - GM-71 | 54 |

NOTE: GM-72 - GM-77 redesignated GP-1 - GP-6 in 1979.
(Refer to 1979 Model 34C)

| T-34C-1 | 1979 | GM-78 | 1 |

NOTE: GM-78 built as Beech factory demonstrator.

T-34C-1	1980	GM-79-GM-81	3
T-34C-1	1981	GM-82 - GM-84	3
T-34C-1	1982	GM-85 - GM-88	3
T-34C-1	1983	GM-1, GM-89	2

NOTE: GM-1 originally built as Beech factory demonstrator in 1977. Sold and delivered in 1983.

| T-34C-1 | 1984 | GM-90 - GM-98 | 9 |

Model 50 Series

50	1952	H-1 - H-11	11
50 (YL-23)	1951	Military prototypes - L-23A series	4
B50	1953	CH-12 - CH-110	99
B50 (U-8D/L-23A)	1952	LH-9 (s/n 52-1801)	1
C50	1954	CH-111 - CH-135	25
C50	1955	CH-136 - CH-351	216
C50	1956	CH-352 - CH-360	9
D50	1956	DH-1 - DH-143	143

NOTE: DH-88 - DH-91 became L-23E.

D50	1956	DH-88 - DH-91 s/n 56-4039, 56-4041, s/n 56-4043, 56-4044	4
D50	1957	DH-144 - DH-154	11
D50A	1958	DH-155 - DH-198	44
D50B	1959	DH-199 - DH-236	38
D50C	1960	DH-237 - DH-300	64
D50E	1961	DH-301 - DH-325	25
D50E	1962	DH-326 - DH-333	8

Model	Year	Constructor Number	Total Delivered
D50E	1963	DH-334 - DH-347	14
E50	1957	EH-1 - EH-70	70
E50 (U-8D)	1957	LH-96 - LH-151 s/n 56-3695 - 56-3718 s/n 57-3084 - 57-3101 s/n 57-6077 - 57-6090	56
E50 (RU-8D)	1957	RLH-1 - RLH-8 s/n 57-6029 - 57-6036	8
E50 (RU-8D)	1958	LH-152 - LH-180 s/n 57-6091 - 57-6094 s/n 58-1329 - 583059	29
E50 (RU-8D)	1958	RLH-9 - RLH-48 s/n 57-6037 - 57-6076 RLH-49 - RLH-60 s/n 58-3048 - 58-3059	52
E50 (RU-8D)	1959	LHC-3 - LHC-10 s/n 58-1357 - 58-1364 LH-192 - LH-195 s/n 59-2535 - 59-2538	12
E50 (RU-8D)	1959	RLH-61 - RLH-93 s/n 58-3060 - 58-3092	33
E50 (U-8G)	1960	LHE-6 - LHE-16 s/n 56-3710, 58-3060 s/n 58-3092, 58-1332 s/n 58-3057, 58-3059 s/n 58-3093, 58-3062 s/n 58-1331, 58-3055 s/n 58-1336	11
F50	1958	FH-71 - FH-93, FH-95, FH-96,	25
G50	1959	GH-94, GH-97 - GH-119	24

NOTE: FH-94 redesignated GH-94.

H50	1960	HH-120 - HH-149	30
J50	1961	JH-150 - JH-161	12
J50	1962	JH-162 - JH-170	9
J50	1963	JH-171 - JH-176	6

NOTE: Model 50 series designated "Twin Bonanza".

Model 95-55 - Model 55 Series

95-55	1961	TC-1 - TC-190	190
95-A55	1962	TC-191 - TC-349, TC-351 - TC-370, TC-372 - TC-379	187
95-A55	1963	TC-380 - TC-501	122
95-B55	1964	TC-371, TC-502 - TC-771	271
95-B55	1965	TC-772 - TC-965	194
B55B (T-42A)	1965	TF-1 - TF-25 s/n 65-12679 - 65-12703	25
95-B55	1966	TC-966 - TC-1016	51
B55B (T-42A)	1966	TF-26 - TF-65 s/n 65-12704 - 65-12733 s/n 66-4300 - 66-4309	40
95-C55	1966	TC-350	1
95-C55	1966	TE-1 - TE-49, TE-51 - TE-266	265
95-B55	1967	TC-1017 - TC-1042	26
95-C55	1967	TE-267 - TE-451	185
95-B55	1968	TC-1043 - TC-1156	114
D55	1968	TE-452 - TE-632	181
95-B55	1969	TC-1157 - TC-1287	131
D55	1969	TE-633 - TE-767	135
95-B55	1970	TC-1288 - TC-1365, TC-1367, TC-1369 - TC-1371	81
E55	1970	TE-768 - TE-824, TE-826, TE-827	59
95-B55	1971	TC-1366, TC-1368, TC-1370, TC-1372 - TC-1401	
B55B (T-42A)	1971	TF-66 - TF-70 s/n 71-21053 - 71-21057	5

NOTE: TF-66 - TF-70 foreign sales. Affected c/n were: TC-1393 (TF-66), TC-1394 (TF-67), TC-1395 (TF-68), TC-1396 (TF-69), TC-1402 (TF-70).

E55	1971	TE-825, TE-828 - TE-846	20
95-B55	1972	TC-1403 - TC-1484	82
E55	1972	TE-847 - TE-879	33
95-B55	1973	TC-1485 - TC-1607	123

MODEL	YEAR	CONSTRUCTOR NUMBER	TOTAL DELIVERED
E55	1973	TE-880 - TE-937, TE-939 - TE-942	62
95-B55	1974	TC-1608 - TC-1781	174
E55	1974	TE-938, TE-943 - TE-1001	60
95-B55	1975	TC-1782 - TC-1905	124
E55	1975	TE-1002 - TE-1064	63
95-B55	1976	TC-1906 - TC-2002	97
E55	1976	TE-1065 - TE-1083	19
95-B55	1977	TC-2003 - TC-2091	89
E55	1977	TE-1084 - TE-1113	30
95-B55	1978	TC-2092 - TC-2180	89
E55	1978	TE-1114 - TE-1142	29
95-B55	1979	TC-2181 - TC-2275	95
E55	1979	TE-1143 - TE-1168	26
95-B55	1980	TC-2276 - TC-2354	79
E55	1980	TE-1169 - TE-1182	14
95-B55	1981	TC-2355 - TC-2420	66
E55	1981	TE-1183 - TE-1195	13
95-B55	1982	TC-2421 - TC-2456	36
E55	1982	TE-1196 - TE-1201	6

NOTE: Model 55 series designated "Baron".

Model 56 Series

MODEL	YEAR	CONSTRUCTOR NUMBER	TOTAL DELIVERED
56TC	1967	TG-2 - TG-51	50
56TC	1968	TG-52 - TG-71	20
56TC	1969	TG-72 - TG-83	12
A56TC	1970	TG-84 - TG-92	9
A56TC	1971	TG-93 - TG-94	2

NOTE: Model 56TC designated "Turbo Baron".

Model 58 Series

MODEL	YEAR	CONSTRUCTOR NUMBER	TOTAL DELIVERED
58	1969	TH-1	1
58	1970	TH-2 - TH-94, TH-96 - TH-98, TH-101 - TH-102	98
58	1971	TH-95, TH-99, TH-100, TH-103 - TH-174	75
58	1972	TH-175 - TH-263	89
58	1973	TH-264 - TH-384	121
58	1974	TH-385 - TH-524	140
58	1975	TH-525 - TH-679	155
58	1976	TH-680 - TH-772	93
58	1977	TH-773 - TH-872	100
58	1978	TH-873 - TH-972	100
58	1979	TH-973 - TH-1079	107
58	1980	TH-1080 - TH-1193	114
58	1981	TH-1194 - TH-1297	104
58	1982	TH-1298 - TH-1355	58
58	1983	TH-1356 - TH-1388, TH-1390 - TH-1395	40
58	1984	TH-1389, TH-1396 - TH-1435	41
58	1985	TH-1436 - TH-1504*	69

*NOTE: The following 1985 Model 58 were converted to 1986 models: TH-1439, TH-1444, TH-1449, TH-1453 - TH-1455, TH-1460, TH-1465, TH-1470, TH-1475, TH-1476, TH-1486, TH-1487, TH-1489 - TH-1491, TH-1494, TH-1498, TH-1501, TH-1503, TH-1505, TH-1506, TH-1507
58 1987 TH-1508 and after

NOTE: Model 58 designated "Baron".

Model 58P Series

MODEL	YEAR	CONSTRUCTOR NUMBER	TOTAL DELIVERED
58P	1976	TJ-3 - TJ-85	83
58P	1977	TJ-86 - TJ-122	37
58P	1978	TJ-123 - TJ-168	46
58P	1979	TJ-169 - TJ-209, TJ-211 - TJ-234	65
58P	1980	TJ-210, TJ-235 - TJ-316	83
58P	1981	TJ-317 - TJ-384	68
58P	1982	TJ-385 - TJ-431	47
58P	1983	TJ-432 - TJ-435, TJ-437 - TJ-443	11
58P	1984	TJ-436, TJ-444 - TJ-470	28
58P	1985	TJ-471 - TJ-497	27

NOTE: Model 58P designated "Pressurized Baron".

Model 58TC Series

MODEL	YEAR	CONSTRUCTOR NUMBER	TOTAL DELIVERED
58TC	1976	TK-1 - TK-34	34
58TC	1977	TK-35 - TK-60	26
58TC	1978	TK-61 - TK-84	24
58TC	1979	TK-85 - TK-109	25
58TC	1980	TK-110 - TK-133	24
58TC	1981	TK-134 - TK-145	12
58TC	1982	TK-146 - TK-149	4
58TC	1983	TK-150	1
58TC	1984	TK-151	1

NOTE: Model 58TC designated "Baron".

Model 60 Series

MODEL	YEAR	CONSTRUCTOR NUMBER	TOTAL DELIVERED
60	1968	P-4 - P-18	15
60	1969	P-19 - P-109	91
60	1970	P-110 - P-122, P-124, P-125, P-126	16
A60	1970	P-123, P-127 - P-139, P-141 - P-146, P-148, P-149, P-151	23
A60	1971	P-140, P-147, P-150, P-152 - P-162, P-167 - P-175, P-178 - P-180, P-182	27
A60	1972	P-163 - P-166, P-176, P-177, P-181, P-183 - P-202, P-210	28
A60	1973	P-203 - P-209, P-211 - P-246	43
B60	1974	P-247 - P-307	61
B60	1975	P-308 - P-347, P-349 - P-364	56
B60	1976	P-348, P-365 - P-401	38
B60	1977	P-402 - P-445	44
B60	1978	P-446 - P-485	40
B60	1979	P-486 - P-510, P-512 - P-519	33
B60	1980	P-511, P-520 - P-555	37
B60	1981	P-556 - P-580	25
B60	1982	P-581 - P-596	16

NOTE: Model 60 series designated "Duke".

Model 65 Series

MODEL	YEAR	CONSTRUCTOR NUMBER	TOTAL DELIVERED
65 (U-8F)	1959	L-3 - L-5 s/n 58-1354 - 58-1356	3
65	1960	L-1, L-2, L-6, LF-7, LF-8, LC-1 - LC-52	56
65 (U-8F)	1960	LF-8 - LF-24 s/n 66-15365, 60-3453 - 60-3463, 60-5386 - 60-5390	17
65	1961	LC-53 - LC-112	60
65 (U-8F)	1961	LF-25 - LF-29 s/n 61-2426 - 61-2430	5
65	1962	LC-113 - LC-147	35
65 (U-8F)	1962	LF-30 - LF-74 s/n 61-3832 - 62-3875, 63-7975	45
65	1963	LC-148 - LC-156	9
65 (U-8F)	1963	LF-75, LF-76 s/n 63-13636, 63-13637	2
65	1964	LC-157 - LC-159	3
65	1965	LC-160 - LC-192	33
65	1966	LC-193 - LC-237	45
65	1967	LC-238, LC-239	2
A65	1967	LC-240 - LC-268	29
A65	1968	LC-269 - LC-272	4
A65-8200*	1968	LC-273 - LC-306	34
A65-8200*	1969	LC-307 - LC-324	18
A65	1969	LC-325 - LC-329	5
A65	1970	LC-330 - LC-335	6

NOTE: Model 65 series designated "Queen Air". *A65-8200 approved for 8,200-pound gross weight.

Model 70 Series

MODEL	YEAR	CONSTRUCTOR NUMBER	TOTAL DELIVERED
70	1969	LB-1 - LB-20	20
70	1970	LB-21 - LB-34	14
70	1971	LB-35	1

NOTE: Model 70 series designated "Queen Air".

MODEL	YEAR	CONSTRUCTOR NUMBER	TOTAL DELIVERED
Model 73			
73	1955	Experimental	1

NOTE: Model 73 "Jet Mentor" was Beech prototype for USAF/U.S. Navy jet trainer competition. Only one built.

Model 76 Series

MODEL	YEAR	CONSTRUCTOR NUMBER	TOTAL DELIVERED
76	1978	ME-1 - ME-72	72
76	1979	ME-73 - ME-282, ME-284 - ME-286	213
76	1980	ME-283, ME-287 - ME-371	86
76	1981	ME-372 - ME-426	55
76	1982	ME-427 - ME-437	11

NOTE: Model 76 designated "Duchess".

Model 77 Series

MODEL	YEAR	CONSTRUCTOR NUMBER	TOTAL DELIVERED
77	1979	WA-1 - WA-47	47
77	1980	WA-48 - WA-187	140
77	1981	WA-188 - WA-312	125

NOTE: Model 77 designated "Skipper".

Model 65-80, 65-A80, 65-B80 Series

MODEL	YEAR	CONSTRUCTOR NUMBER	TOTAL DELIVERED
65-80	1962	LD-1 - LD-33, LD-35 - LD-45, LD-47 - LD-55	53
65-80	1963	LD-56 - LD-150	95
65-A80*	1964	LD-34, LD-46, LD-151 - LD-193	45
65-A80*	1965	LD-194 - LD-249	56
65-A80*	1966	LD-250 - LD-269	20

NOTE: 65-A80 series designated "Queen Air". *A65-A80 approved for 8,800-pound gross weight.

MODEL	YEAR	CONSTRUCTOR NUMBER	TOTAL DELIVERED
65-B80	1966	LD-270 - LD-313	44
65-B80	1967	LD-314 - LD-361	48
65-B80	1968	LD-362 - LD-405	44
65-B80	1969	LD-406 - LD-425	20
65-B80	1970	LD-426 - LD-433, LD-437, LD-439, LD-441	11
65-B80	1971	LD-434, LD-435, LD-436, LD-438, LD-440, LD-442 - LD-447	11
65-B80	1972	LD-448 - LD-460	13
65-B80	1973	LD-461 - LD-472	12
65-B80	1974	LD-473 - LD-487	15
65-B80	1975	LD-488 - LD-505	18
65-B80	1976	LD-506, LD-507	2
65-B80	1977	LD-508 - LD-511	4

NOTE: Model 65-B80 designated "Queen Air".

Model 87

MODEL	YEAR	CONSTRUCTOR NUMBER	TOTAL DELIVERED
87 (NU-8F)	1963	LG-1 s/n 63-12902	1

NOTE: Prototype for U-21 series, designated YU-21.

Model 65-88 Series

MODEL	YEAR	CONSTRUCTOR NUMBER	TOTAL DELIVERED
65-88	1965	LP-1 - LP-4	4
65-88	1966	LP-5 - LP-26, LP-28, LP-30 - LP-40	34

NOTE: LP-27 converted to LJ-178A, LP-29 converted to LJ-116. Both airplanes equipped with PT6A-6 turboprop engine installation similar to Model 65-90 King Air.

MODEL	YEAR	CONSTRUCTOR NUMBER	TOTAL DELIVERED
65-88	1967	LP-41 - LP-45	5
65-88	1968	LP-46	1
65-88	1969	LP-47	1

NOTE: 65-88 series originally designated Model 85, but were produced as Model 65-88 Queen Air. It was the first production piston-engine Beechcraft to feature a pressurized cabin.

Model 65-90 Series

MODEL	YEAR	CONSTRUCTOR NUMBER	TOTAL DELIVERED
65-90	1964	LJ-1 - LJ-7	7
65-90	1965	LJ-8 - LJ-75, LJ-77	69
65-90	1966	LJ-78-LJ-113	36
65-A90	1966	LJ-114 - LJ-183, LJ-76, LJ-178A	72
65-A90	1967	LJ-184 - LJ-317	134

NOTE: 65-90 - 65-A90 series designated "King Air".

MODEL	YEAR	CONSTRUCTOR NUMBER	TOTAL DELIVERED
A90-1 (U-21A)	1967	LM-1 - LM-77 s/n 66-18000 - 67-18076 LM-78 - LM-84 s/n 67-18078 - 67-18084 LM-85, LM-86 s/n 67-18086 - 67-18088 LM-87 - LM-89 s/n 67-18090 - 67-18092 LM-90, LM-91 s/n 67-18094 - 67-18095	91
A90-2 (RU-21B)	1967	LS-1 - LS-3 s/n 67-18077, 67-18087 67-18093	3
A90-3 (RU-21C)	1967	LT-1, LT-2 s/n 67-18085, 67-18089	2
A90-1 (U-21A)	1968	LM-92 - LM-99 s/n 67-18096 - 67-18103 LM-115 - LM-117 s/n 67-18116 - 67-18118	11
A90-1 (RU-21A)	1968	LM-108 - LM-111 s/n 67-18112 - 67-18115	4
A90-1 (RU-21D)	1968	LM-100 - LM-107 s/n 67-18104 - 67-18111 LM-115 - LM-117 s/n 67-18119 - 67-18121	10
A90-1 (RU-21D)	1969	LM-118 - LM-124 s/n 67-18122 - 67-18128	7
A90-1 (U-21G)	1971	LM-125 - LM-141 s/n 70-15891 - 70-15907	17
A90-4 (RU-21E) (RU-21H)	1971	LU-1 - LU-16 s/n 70-15875 - 70-15890	16

Model B90 Series

MODEL	YEAR	CONSTRUCTOR NUMBER	TOTAL DELIVERED
B90	1968	LJ-318 - LJ-408	91
B90	1969	LJ-409 - LJ-481	73
B90	1970	LJ-482 - LJ-501	20

NOTE: Model B90 series designated "King Air".

Model C90 Series

MODEL	YEAR	CONSTRUCTOR NUMBER	TOTAL DELIVERED
C90	1971	LJ-502 - LJ-533	32
C90	1972	LJ-534 - LJ-567	34
C90	1973	LJ-568 - LJ-608	41
C90	1974	LJ-609 - LJ-641	33
C90	1975	LJ-642 - LJ-673	32
C90	1976	LJ-674 - LJ-701	28
C90	1977	LJ-702 - LJ-741	40
C90	1978	LJ-742 - LJ-802	61
C90	1979	LJ-803 - LJ-869	67
C90	1980	LJ-870 - LJ-925	56
C90	1981	LJ-926 - LJ-985, LJ-987 - LJ-993	67
C90	1982	LJ-994, LJ-995, LJ-997 - LJ-1010	16
C90-1	1982	LJ-986, LJ-996, LJ-1011 - LJ-1044, LJ-1047	37
C90-1	1983	LJ-1045, LJ-1046, LJ-1048 - LJ-1062	17
C90A	1984	LJ-1063 - LJ-1084, LJ-1086 - LJ-1087	24

MODEL	YEAR	CONSTRUCTOR NUMBER	TOTAL DELIVERED
C90A	1985	LJ-1085, LJ-1088 - LJ-1127	41
C90A	1986	LJ-1128 - LJ-1137	9
C90A	1987	LJ-1138 and after*	

*NOTE: LJ-1138 is prototype for C90A with gross weight increase.

NOTE: Model C90 series designated "King Air".

Model E90 Series

MODEL	YEAR	CONSTRUCTOR NUMBER	TOTAL DELIVERED
E90	1972	LW-1 - LW-16, LW-18 - LW-23	22
E90	1973	LW-17, LW-24 - LW-73	51
E90	1974	LW-74 - LW-117	44
E90	1975	LW-118 - LW-156	39
E90	1976	LW-157 - LW-201	45
E90	1977	LW-202 - LW-251	50
E90	1978	LW-252 - LW-301	50
E90	1979	LW-302 - LW-327	26
E90	1980	LW-328 - LW-341	14
E90	1981	LW-342 - LW-347	6

NOTE: Model E90 designated "King Air".

Model F90 Series

MODEL	YEAR	CONSTRUCTOR NUMBER	TOTAL DELIVERED
F90	1979	LA-2 - LA-8	7

NOTE: LA-1 converted to LE-0 for experimental work.

MODEL	YEAR	CONSTRUCTOR NUMBER	TOTAL DELIVERED
F90	1980	LA-9 - LA-81	73
F90	1981	LA-82 - LA-156	75
F90	1982	LA-157 - LA-183, LA-185 - LA-197, LA-199	41
F90	1983	LA-184, LA-198, LA-200, LA-201, LA-203, LA-204	6
F90-1	1983	LA-202, LA-205 - LA-214	11
F90-1	1984	LA-215 - LA-225	11
F90-1	1985	LA-226 - LA-236	11
F90-1	1986	LA-237	1

NOTE: F90 - F90-1 series designated "King Air".

Model H90

NOTE: Model H90 was produced for the U.S. Navy with military designation T-44A, not equivalent to any King Air. None were built for commercial sale. The c/n and military serial number are presented:

MODEL	YEAR	CONSTRUCTOR NUMBER	TOTAL DELIVERED
H90	1977	LL-1 - LL-13 s/n 160839 - 160851	13
H90	1978	LL-14 - LL-35 s/n 160852 - 160856, s/n 160967 - 160983	21
H90	1979	LL-36 - LL-58 s/n 160984 - 160986, s/n 161057 - 161076	23
H90	1980	LL-59 - LL-61 s/n 161077 - 161079	3

Model 95 Series

MODEL	YEAR	CONSTRUCTOR NUMBER	TOTAL DELIVERED
95	1958	TD-2 - TD-173, TD-185	173
95	1959	TD-174 - TD-184, TD-186 - TD-302	128
B95	1960	TD-303 - TD-452	150
B95A	1961	TD-453 - TD-491	39
B95A	1962	TD-492 - TD-533	42
D95A	1963	TD-534 - TD-552	19
D95A	1964	TD-553 - TD-592	40
D95A	1965	TD-593 - TD-640	48
D95A	1966	TD-641 - TD-673	33
D95A	1967	TD-674 - TD-707	34
E95	1968	TD-708 - TD-721	14

NOTE: Model 95 series designated "Travel Air".

Model 99 Series

MODEL	YEAR	CONSTRUCTOR NUMBER	TOTAL DELIVERED
99	1968	U-1 - U-35, U-37 - U-45	44
99A	1968	U-36	1

NOTE: U-36 was Beech factory demonstrator. Sold 9-30-71.

MODEL	YEAR	CONSTRUCTOR NUMBER	TOTAL DELIVERED
99	1969	U-46 - U-49, U-51 - U-79, U-86 - U-88, U-90 - U-92, U-94, U-95, U-98, U-99, U-100, U-102, U-103, U-106 - U-109, U-114, U-119 - U-122, U-124	56

NOTE: U-50 was Model 99, became prototype C99 in 1980.

MODEL	YEAR	CONSTRUCTOR NUMBER	TOTAL DELIVERED
99A	1969	U-80 - U-85, U-89, U-93, U-96, U-97, U-101, U-104, U-105, U-110 - U-113, U-115 - U-118, U-123, U-125 - U-127	25
99	1970	U-136	1
99A	1970	U-128 - U-131, U-133 - U-135, U-137 - U-145	16
A99A	1970	U-132	1
99A	1971	U-147	1
B99	1972	U-146, U-148, U-150, U-151	4

NOTE: U-148 sold 11-24-71 as 99A. Modifed to B99 7-14-72 at Beech factory.

MODEL	YEAR	CONSTRUCTOR NUMBER	TOTAL DELIVERED
B99	1973	U-149	1
B99	1974	U-152 - U-159	8
B99	1975	U-160 - U-164	5
C99	1982	U-50, U-165 - U-203	40
C99	1983	U-204 - U-216	13
C99	1984	U-217 - U-227	11
C99	1985	U-228 - U-233	6
C99	1986	U-234 - U-239	6
C99	1987	U-240 and after	

NOTE: Model 99 series designated "Airliner".

Model 100 - A100 - B100 Series

MODEL	YEAR	CONSTRUCTOR NUMBER	TOTAL DELIVERED
100	1969	B-2 - B-8	7

NOTE: B-1 was originally a Model 100, changed to Model A100 in fiscal year 1976.

MODEL	YEAR	CONSTRUCTOR NUMBER	TOTAL DELIVERED
100	1970	B-9 - B-65, B-68, B-70 B-72	60
100	1971	B-66, B-67, B-69, B-71, B-73 - B-89, B-93	22
A100	1972	B-90, B-91, B-92, B-94 - B-135, B-137, B-138	47
A100 (U-21F)	1971	B-95 - B-99 s/n 70-15908 - 70-15912	5
A100	1973	B-136, B-139 - B-177	40
A100	1974	B-178 - B-204	27
A100	1975	B-206 - B-222	17

NOTE: B-205 became Model B100 prototype BE-1.

MODEL	YEAR	CONSTRUCTOR NUMBER	TOTAL DELIVERED
A100	1976	B-1, B-223 - B-230	9
A100	1977	B-231 - B237	7
A100	1978	B-238 - B-240, B-242	4
A100	1979	B-241, B-243 - B-247	6
B100	1976	BE-1 - BE-16	16
B100	1977	BE-17 - BE-31	15
B100	1978	BE-32 - BE-54	23
B100	1979	BE-55 - BE-77	23
B100	1980	BE-78 - BE-102	25
B100	1981	BE-103 - BE-122	20
B100	1982	BE-123 - BE-132, BE-135	11
B100	1983	BE-133, BE-134, BE-136, BE-137	4

MODEL	YEAR	CONSTRUCTOR NUMBER	TOTAL DELIVERED
Model 200 - B200 Series			
A100-1 (RU-21J) (U.S. Army)	1972	BB-3 - BB-5 s/n 71-21058 - 71-21060	3
200	1974	BB-2 - BB-17	13

NOTE: BB-1 was engineering prototype. BB-2 was Beech factory demonstrator.

MODEL	YEAR	CONSTRUCTOR NUMBER	TOTAL DELIVERED
200	1975	BB-18 - BB-88	71
A200 (C12A) (U.S. Army)	1975	BC-1 - BC-8 s/n 73-22250 - 73-22257 BC-9 - BC-10 s/n 73-22261, 73-22262	20
(U.S. Air Force)		BD-1 - BD-10 s/n 73-1205 - 73-1214	
200	1976	BB-89 - BB-185 BB-187, BB-188	99

NOTE: BB-186 became BT-1 with wing tip tanks in 1976.

MODEL	YEAR	CONSTRUCTOR NUMBER	TOTAL DELIVERED
A200 (C-12A) (U.S. Army)	1976	BC-11 - BC-13 s/n 73-22263 - 73-22265 BC-14 - BC-16 s/n 73-22258 - 73-22260 BC-17 - BC-2 s/n 73-22266 - 73-22269 BC-21, BC-22 s/n 76-22245 - 76-22246	32
(U.S. Air Force)		BD-11 - BD-14 s/n 73-1215 - 73-1218 BD-15 - BD-26 s/n 76-0158 - 76-0169 BD-27 - BD-30 s/n 76-0173, 76-0171, 76-0172, 76-0170	
200	1977	BB-189 - BB-202, BB-204 - BB-269, BB-271 - BB-300	110
A200 (C-12A) (U.S. Army)	1977	BC-23 - BC-33 s/n 76-22547 - 76-22557 BC-34, BC-35 - BC-41 s/n 76-22951, 76-22558 - 76-22564	19
200	1978	BB-301 - BB-407 BB-409 - BB-414	113
A200 (C-12A) (U.S. Army)	1978	BC-42 - BC-61 s/n 77-22931 - 77-22950	20
200	1979	BB-415 - BB-468, BB-470 - BB-488, BB-490 - BB-509, BB-511 - BB-529, BB-531 - BB-550, BB-552 - BB-562, BB-564 - BB-572	152
A200 (C-12C) (U.S. Army)	1979	BC-62 - BC-75 s/n 78-23126 - 78-23139	14
A200C (UC-12B) (U.S. Navy)	1979	BJ-1 - BJ-9 s/n 16-1185 - 16-1193	9
200	1980	BB-574 - BB-590, BB-592 - BB-608, BB-610 - BB-626, BB-628 - BB-646, B-648 - BB-664, BB-666 - BB-694, BB-696 - BB-733, BB-735 - BB-747	149
A200C (UC-12B) (U.S. Navy)	1980	BJ-10 - BJ-36 s/n 16-1194 - 16-1206 16-1306 - 16-1319	27
A200CT (C-12D) (U.S. Army)	1980	BP-1 - BP-6 s/n 78-23140 - 78-23145	6

MODEL	YEAR	CONSTRUCTOR NUMBER	TOTAL DELIVERED
200	1981	BB-734, BB-748 - BB-792, BB-794 - BB-797, BB-799 - BB-822, BB-824 - BB-828, BB-830 - BB-853, BB-872, BB-873, BB-892, BB-893, BB-912	108
A200C (UC-12B) (U.S. Navy)	1981	BJ-37 - BJ-58 s/n 16-1320 - 16-1327, 16-1497 - 16-1510	22
A200CT (C-12D) (U.S. Army)	1981	BP-7 - BP-11 BP-12 - BP-21 s/n 80-23371 - 80-23380	15

NOTE: BP-7 - BP-11 foreign sales.

MODEL	YEAR	CONSTRUCTOR NUMBER	TOTAL DELIVERED
B200	1981	BB-793, BB-829, BB-854 - BB-870, BB-874 - BB-891, BB-894, BB-896 - BB-911, BB-913 - BB-923, BB-925- BB-942*	83

*NOTE: BB-870 built as BL-36 with PT6A-41 engines. BB-871 built as BT-20 with PT6A-41 engines. BB-872 and BB-873 built with PT6A-41 engines. BB-892 and BB-893 built with PT6A-41 engines. BB-895 built as BT-21 with PT6A-41 engines. BB-912 built with PT6A-41 engines.

MODEL	YEAR	CONSTRUCTOR NUMBER	TOTAL DELIVERED
B200	1982	BB-924, BB-943 - BB-990, BB-992 - BB-1050, BB-1053 - BB-1090	147
A200C (UC-12B) (U.S. Navy)	1982	BJ-59 - BJ-66 s/n 16-1511 - 16-1518	8
A200C (UC-12F) (U.S. Navy)	1986	BU-1 - BU-12	12

NOTE: BU-11 and BU-12 modified by Beech for "RANSAC" firing range surveillance duty.

MODEL	YEAR	CONSTRUCTOR NUMBER	TOTAL DELIVERED
A200C (UC-12M) (U.S. Navy)	1987-88	BV-1 - BV-12	12
A200CT (C-12D) (U.S. Army)	1982	BP-22 - BP-27 s/n 81-23541 - 81-23546	6
B200	1983	BB-1051, BB-1091, BB-1092, BB-1094, BB-1095, BB-1099 - BB-1104, BB-1106 - BB-1116, BB-1118 - BB-1152, BB-1154 - BB-1156, BB-1159 - BB-1166	63
A200CT (C-12D) (U.S. Army)	1983	BP-28 - BP-34 s/n 82-23780 - 82-23785, 83-24145	7
A200CT (RC-12D) (U.S. Army)	1983	GR-1, GR-3 s/n 81-23542, 80-23377	2
B200	1984	BB-1153, BB-1157, BB-1168 - BB-1192	27
B200C (C-12F) (U.S. Air Force)	1984	BL-73 - BL-112 s/n 84-0143 - 84-0182	38
A200CT (C-12D) (U.S. Army)	1984	BP-35 - BP-39 s/n 83-24146 - 83-24150 BP-40 - BP-45 s/n 83-0494 - 83-0499	11
A200CT (C-12F) (U.S. Army)	1986	BP-51 - BP-69	19
A200CT (RC-12D) (U.S. Army)	1984	GR-2, GR-4 - GR-13 s/n 80-23371, 80-23373, 80-23375, 78-23141 - 78-23145, 80-23376, 80-23374, 80-23378	11
A200CT (U.S. Army)	1986-87	GR-14 - GR-19	6
A200CT (RC-12D) (U.S. Army)	1984	FC-1 - FC-3 s/n 80-23379, 80-23380, 80-23372	3

MODEL	YEAR	CONSTRUCTOR NUMBER	TOTAL DELIVERED
A200CT (RC-12K) (U.S. Army)	1986-87	FE-1 - FE-9	9
B200	1985	BB-1158, BB-1167, BB-1193 - BB-1242	52
B200	1986	BB-1243 - BB-1260	17
B200	1987	BB-1261 and after	

NOTE: Model 200 - B200 series designated "Super King Air".

Model 200C - B200C Series

NOTE: Model 200C and B200C equipped with cargo door.

MODEL	YEAR	CONSTRUCTOR NUMBER	TOTAL DELIVERED
200C	1979	BL-1 - BL-4	4
200C	1980	BL-5 - BL-13	9
200C	1981	BL-14 - BL-23, BL-25 - BL-36	22
B200C	1981	BL-37 - BL-43	7
B200C	1982	BL-44 - BL-57	14
B200C	1983	BL-61 - BL-71	11
B200C (C-12F) (U.S. Air Force)	1984	BL-72 - BL-123*	47

*NOTE: BL-73 - BL-112 assigned as C-12F for U.S. Air Force OSA program. BL-113 - BL-117 were not built. Six additional C-12F were built for Air National Guard units and assigned c/n BL-118 - BL-123. BL-73 - BL-112 delivered under lease, converted to sales in 12-86.

MODEL	YEAR	CONSTRUCTOR NUMBER	TOTAL DELIVERED
B200C	1985	BL-124 - BL-126	3
B200C	1986	BL-127	1
B200C	1987	BL-128, BL-129	2

Model 200T/200CT - B200T/B200CT Series

NOTE: Model 200CT and B200CT equipped with cargo door and wing tip tanks. Numbers in parentheses indicate original c/n before reassignment as 200CT and B200CT:

MODEL	YEAR	CONSTRUCTOR NUMBER	TOTAL DELIVERED
200CT	1981	BN-1 (BL-24)	1
B200CT	1982	BN-2 (BL-58)	1
B200CT	1983	BN-3 (BL-59), BN-4 (BL-60)	2

Model 200T - B200T Series

NOTE: Model 200T and B200T equipped with wing tip tanks.

MODEL	YEAR	CONSTRUCTOR NUMBER	TOTAL DELIVERED
200T	1976	BT-1 (BB-186)	1
200T	1977	BT-2 (BB-203), BT-3 (BB-270)	2
200T	1978	BT-4 (BB-408)	1
200T	1979	BT-5 (BB-469), BT-6 (BB-489), BT-7 (BB-510), BT-8 (BB-530), BT-9 (BB-551), BT-10 (BB-563), BT-11 (BB-573)	7
200T	1980	BT-12 (BB-591), BT-13 (BB-609), BT-14 (BB-627), BT-15 (BB-647), BT-16 (BB-665), BT-17 (BB-687), BT-18 (BB-695)	10
200T	1981	BT-19 (BB-823), BT-20 (BB-871), BT-21 (BB-895)	3
200T	1982	BT-22 (BB-991)	1
200T	1983	BT-28 (BB-1117)	1
B200T	1982	BT-23 (BB-1052)	1
B200T	1983	BT-24 (BB-1093), BT-25 (BB-1096), BT-26 (BB-1098), BT-27 (BB-1105), BT-29 (BB-1097)	5
B200T	1984	BT-30 (BB-1185)	1
B200T	1987	BT-31 (BB-1264)	1

NOTE: Model 200T - B200T designated "Super King Air". No BT series produced in 1985-1986 calendar years.

Model 300

MODEL	YEAR	TOTAL CONSTRUCTOR NUMBER	DELIVERED
300	1984	FA-1 - FA-27	27
300	1985	FA-28 - FA-87	60
300	1986	FA-88 - FA-111	23
300	1987	FA-112 and after	
300	1987-88	FF-1 - FF-19*	19

*NOTE: FF-1 - FF-19 sold to Federal Aviation Administration with deliveries beginning in 1987 through 1988. Model 300 modified for national airway/navigation system surveillance.

NOTE: Model 300 designated "Super King Air".

Model 400

MODEL	YEAR	TOTAL CONSTRUCTOR NUMBER	DELIVERED
400	1986	RJ-3, RJ-9 - RJ-16	8
400	1987	RJ-17 and after	

NOTE: Model 400 designated "Beechjet".

Model 1900 Series

MODEL	YEAR	TOTAL CONSTRUCTOR NUMBER	DELIVERED
1900	1983	UA-2, UA-3	2
1900C	1984	UB-1 - UB-28	28
1900C	1985	UB-29 - UB-50	22
1900C	1986	UB-51 - UB-66	15
1900C	1987	UB-67 and after	
1900C-1	1987	UC-1 and after*	

*NOTE: Model 1900C-1 c/n UC-1 and after equipped with 670-gallon integral(wet) wing fuel system. All Model 1900 and Model 1900C are designated "1900 Airliner" except executive version designated "King Air Exec-Liner".

MODEL	YEAR	TOTAL CONSTRUCTOR NUMBER	DELIVERED
1900C-1 (C-12J)	1987	UD-1 - UD-6	6

NOTE: UD-1 - UD-6 for U.S. Army National Guard units. Equipped with 670-gallon integral (wet) wing fuel system.

Keeping the trainers ready for day-long operations required night work in the hangars at Hondo Field, Texas. These AT-7's housed navigation instruments including an astrodome in the roof. (Photo from Ed Kueppers collection).

1. Walter Beech leased two buildings of the Cessna Aircraft Company's factory to build the first Beechcraft biplanes. Cessna's Board of Directors approved the lease but Clyde Cessna himself was not involved with the transaction nor the firm that bore his name in April, 1932. Cessna and his son, Eldon, had formed their own airplane company and were building specialized racers in a small facility near the Stearman plant in south Wichita. Later, in 1933, the Cessnas were building famed racing pilot Johnny Livingston's CR-3 in the ex-Travel Air facility before Beech transferred production there during the spring of 1934. Although Ted Wells was responsible for the Model 17R's design, he received valuable assistance from co-engineers Jack Wassal, Cecil Barlow, Wayne Dalrymple, Harry Soderstrom and Willard Bashshaw.

2. Two Model 17R were built, c/n 1 and c/n 2. Both were manufactured in the Cessna factory. Welded steel tube, truss-type spars were used with wood ribs and fabric covering over the wings. Because of persistant cracks and breakage of the streamlined steel brace wires on the empennage, steel tubing was substituted and worked well on c/n 2, NC58Y, as did the full-swiveling tailwheel that greatly improved ground handling characteristics. First 17R, NC499N, also received full-swiveling tailwheel before delivery to Ethyl Corporation.

3. The A17FS was originally built for the MacRobertson Race, to be flown by Robert Fogg and Louise McPhetridge von Thaden. However, it was withdrawn prior to the event and sold to the Civil Aeronautics Authority, who flew the 710 hp A17FS several years before it was reportedly dismantled around 1937.

4. Beechcrafter Virgil Adamson sailed to Japan and assisted the Japanese in assembly of the two C17E biplanes. Beech's first amphibian, the SC17B, handled well on water but poorly on land because the trailing edge of the floats dragged on the ground, making turns very difficult. The project was eventually abandoned but was a worthwhile experiment.

5. The Model G17S was virtually a hand-built flying machine. It took hundreds of man-hours to construct its intricate spruce fairings, weld its steel tube fuselage and fabricate its wooden wings. Labor costs were simply too high after the war to achieve economical production. The basic design of the Staggerwing did not lend itself to adoption of mass production techniques, further discouraging its future. At $29,000, the G17S could not hope to compete with the all-metal, swift and modern Model 35 Bonanza that sold for only $7,975 in 1946.

6. Ted Wells and Walter Beech were aware of the Lockheed Model 12 transport that featured twin tails, but they wanted their airplane to be slightly smaller. Although stories have circulated over the years that Beech simply copied the Lockheed design, there is no evidence to that effect and it seems quite unlikely since men like Wells and Beech needed no inspiration from other designers to be innovative. The most substantial reason for the Model 18 possessing two vertical stabilizers can be traced to the art of stress analysis in the mid-1930s. Ted Wells was thoroughly familiar with analysis of steel tube truss-type structures. He had been working with them for 10 years by 1936, but the all-metal, semi-monocoque structure of the Model 18 presented some unique and difficult problems for stress analysis, particularly because Wells and his tiny staff had virtually no experience with all-metal airframes. A single, conventional vertical stabilizer could have been used on the new Beechcraft, but there was one glitch: the torsional stresses imposed on the aft fuselage under single-engine conditions proved to be a somewhat nebulous phenomenon, not fully understood by many aeronautical engineers of the day. To avoid problems with analyzing such stresses and to ensure a safe design, Wells elected to use two tails...a configuration that would make stress analysis (and therefore certification) an easier task. Mounting the two tails outboard retained the total area needed to maintain directional control on one engine and proved to be the best overall configuration.

7. Exactly how many Model 18 were built from 1937 to 1969 is uncertain. Beech Aircraft Corporation claims 5,680 airplanes were built during World War Two and 1,861 commercial units were produced for a grand total of 7,541. However, other records indicate that 1,914 commercial Model 18 were built from 1946 to 1969. When these are added to the prewar number of 202 airplanes indicated by Beech records, plus war production the grand total is 7,796. Most historians agree that somewhere between 7,000 and 8,000 Model 18 were produced so the 7,796 figure may be reasonably accurate.

8. The Model 34 Twin Quad was not the first airplane to use two engines mounted in the wings driving a single propeller. The German Heinkel He 177 long-range, heavy bomber used a very similar installation during World War Two. Like the Twin Quad, the He 177 featured two engines coupled together driving a single propeller through a reduction gearbox. Engines were Daimler-Benz DB 606A developing 2,700 hp each.

9. The following list gives Beech constructor number for the six USAF L-23E airplanes according to Beech records. Commercial equivalent was Model D50:

L-23E	c/n DH-2	Delivered April, 1956
L-23E	c/n DH-18	Delivered April, 1956
L-23E	c/n DH-79	Delivered May, 1956
L-23E	c/n DH-80	Delivered June, 1956
L-23E	c/n DH-90	Delivered July, 1956
L-23E	c/n DH-91	Delivered July, 1956

10. Certain Model 58TC and Model 58P airplanes were reworked in the field by Beech service engineering teams. Beech Kit #102-5010 was installed that increased gross weight of both models from 6,100 pounds to 6,200 pounds. The kit also provided modifications that changed engine horsepower from 310 to 325 hp, redesignating the powerplants as TSIO-520-LB1C WB1. The modified airplanes were: Model 58TC: c/n TK-85 -c/n TK-91; Model 58P: c/n TJ-169 - c/n TJ-192.

11. The following list contains Beech constructor number and military serial number for the L-23/U-8-series Model 50 Twin Bonanza and U-8F-series Model 65 Queen Air:

YEAR	MODEL	BEECH C/N	MILITARY S/N
1952	L-23B/U-8D	LH-9	52-1801
1956	L-23E/U-8D	DH-88 - DH-91	56-4039, 56-4041,
			56-4043, 56-4044
1957	L-23D/U-8D	LH-96 - LH-151	56-3695 - 56-3718
			57-3084 - 57-3101
			57-6077 - 57-6090
1957	RL-23D/RU-8D	RLH-1 - RLH-8	57-6029 - 57-6036
1958	L-23D/U-8D	LH-152 - LH-180	57-6091 - 57-6094
			58-1329 - 58-3059
1958	RL-23D/RU-8D	RLH-9 - RLH-48	57-6037 - 57-6076
		RLH-49 - RLH-60	58-3048 - 58-3059
1959	RU-8D	LHC-3 - LHC-10	58-1357 - 58-1364
		LH-192 - LH-195	59-2535 - 59-2538
1959	RU-8D	RLH-61 - RLH-93	58-3060 - 58-3092
1959	U-8F	L-3 - L-5	58-1354 - 58-1356
1960	U-8G	LHE-6 - LHE-16	56-3710, 58-3060,
			58-3092, 58-1332,
			58-3057, 58-3059,
			58-3093, 58-3062,

			58-1331, 58-3055, 58-1336
1960	U-8F	LF-8 - LF-24	60-3453 - 60-3463
			60-5386 - 60-5390
			66-15365
1961	U-8F	LF-25 - LF-29	61-2426 - 61-2430
1962	U-8F	LF-30 - LF-74	61-3832 - 62-3875
			63-7975
1963	U-8F	LF-75, LF-76	63-13636
			63-13637
1963	NU-8F/YU-21	LG-1 63-12902	

NOTE: LG-1 was first turboprop U-8, with two PT6-6 engines.

12. The following list contains Beech constructor numbers and military serial numbers for the A90-1 - A90-4-series Model 90 King Air and U-21F Model A100 King Air:

1967	A90-1/U-21A	LM-1 - LM-77	66-18000 - 66-18076
		LM-78 - LM-84	67-18078 - 67-18084
		LM-85, LM-86	67-18086, 67-18088
		LM-87 - LM-89	67-18090 - 67-18092
		LM-90 - LM-91	67-18094 - 67-18095
1967	A90-2/RU-21B	LS-1 - LS-3	67-18077, 67-18087
			67-18093
1967	A90-3/RU-21C	LT-1, LT-2	67-18085, 67-18089
1968	A90-1/U-21A	LM-92 - LM-99	67-18096 - 67-18103
		LM-112 - LM-114	67-18116 - 67-18118
1968	A90-1/RU-21A	LM-108 - LM-111	67-18112 - 67-18115
1968	A90-1/RU-21D	LM-100 - LM-107	67-18104 - 67-18111
		LM-115 - LM-117	67-18119 - 67-18121
1969	A90-1/RU-21D	LM-118 - LM-124	67-18122 - 67-18128
1971	A90-1/U-21G	LM-125 - LM-141	70-15891 - 70-15907
1971	A90-4/RU-21E RU-21H	LU-1 - LU-16	70-15875 - 70-15890
1971	U-21F	B-95 - B-99	70-15908 - 70-15912

ARCHIVAL RECORDS

1. Beech Aircraft Corporation (A Raytheon Company): production records, constructor number files, company archives, marketing and engineering data from 1932 to 1987.

HISTORICAL AND TECHNICAL PUBLICATIONS

1. Ball, Larry A.: Those Incomparable Bonanzas; McCormick-Armstrong Co.; 1971.

2. Christy, Joe; The Complete Guide To Single-Engine Beechcrafts; TAB Books; 1979.

3. McDaniel, William H. and Beech Aircraft Corporation; The History of Beech; McCormick-Armstrong Co.; 1982.

4. Smith, Robert T. and Lempicke, Thomas A.; Staggerwing!; Cody Publications; 1979.

AT-7 just off the ground from Hondo Field, Texas with the gear beginning to go up. (Ed Kueppers collection).

Interior of AT-7 "Navigator" showing the three student seats and the overhead astrodome through which celestial readings were taken. (Ed Kueppers collection).

Excellent view of the astrodome on an AT-7. All photos in this series were taken by Bernard W. Gouette for the Army Air Force News Service. (Ed Kueppers collection).

Interior view of AT-7 looking forward. Student positions as well as the cockpit are visible. Oxygen bottles and parachute await the students at Hondo, Texas. (Ed Kueppers collection).

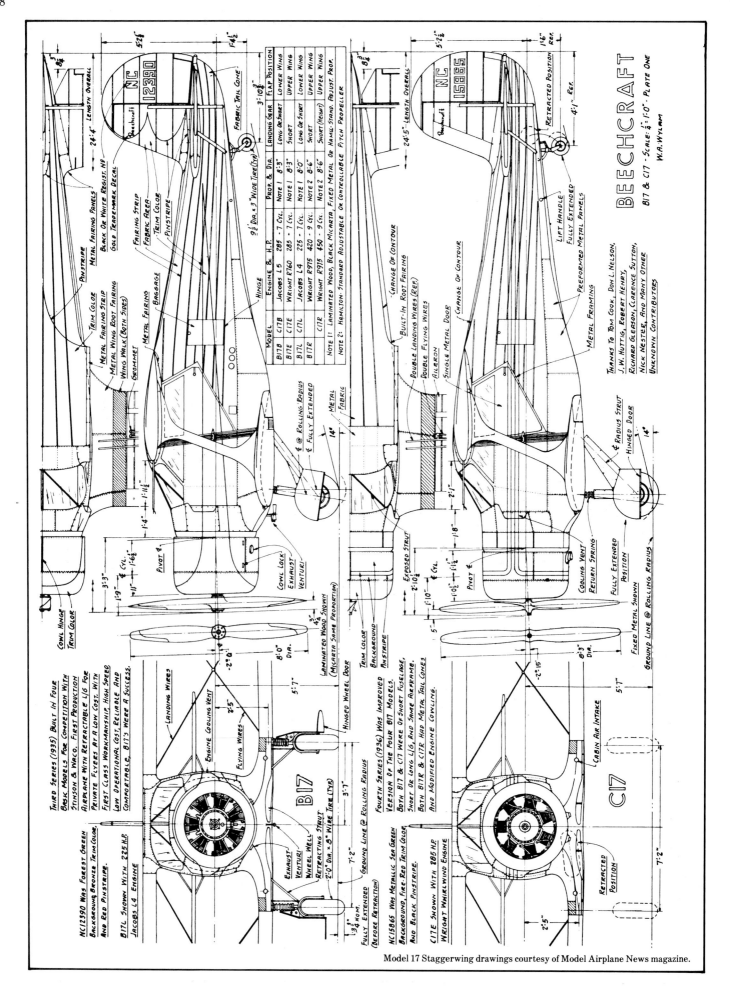

Model 17 Staggerwing drawings courtesy of Model Airplane News magazine.

89

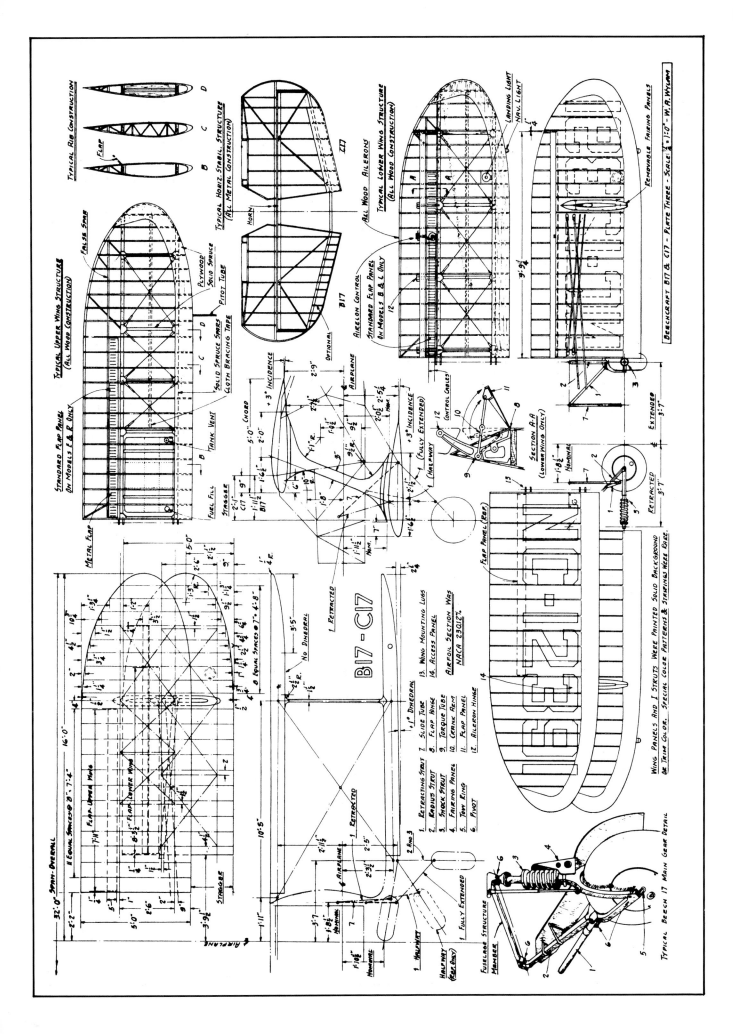

90

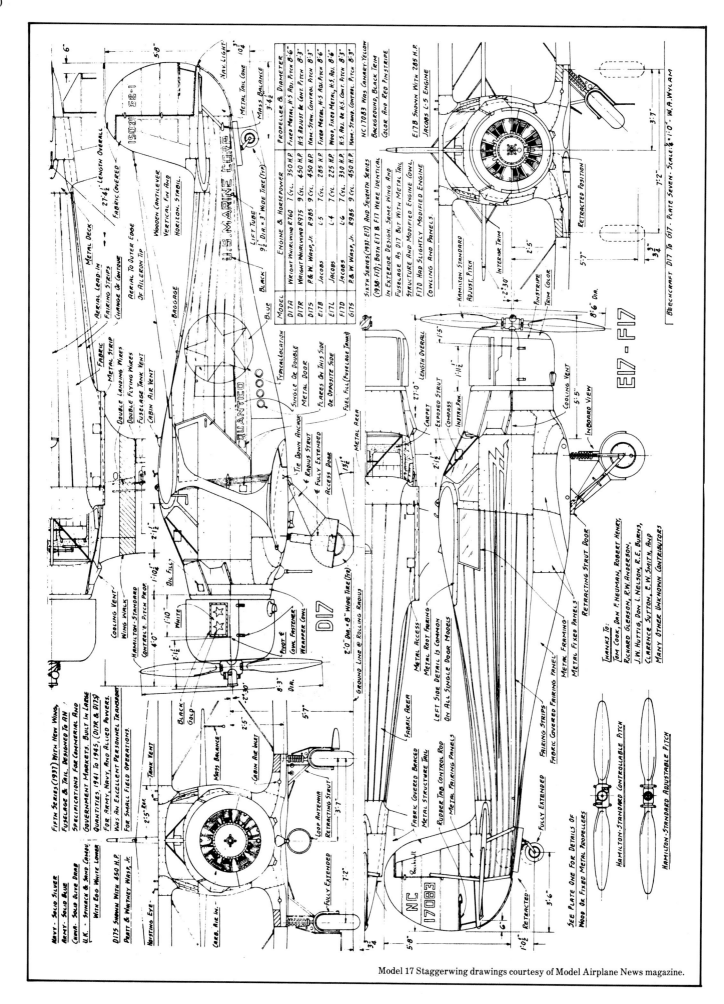

Model 17 Staggerwing drawings courtesy of Model Airplane News magazine.

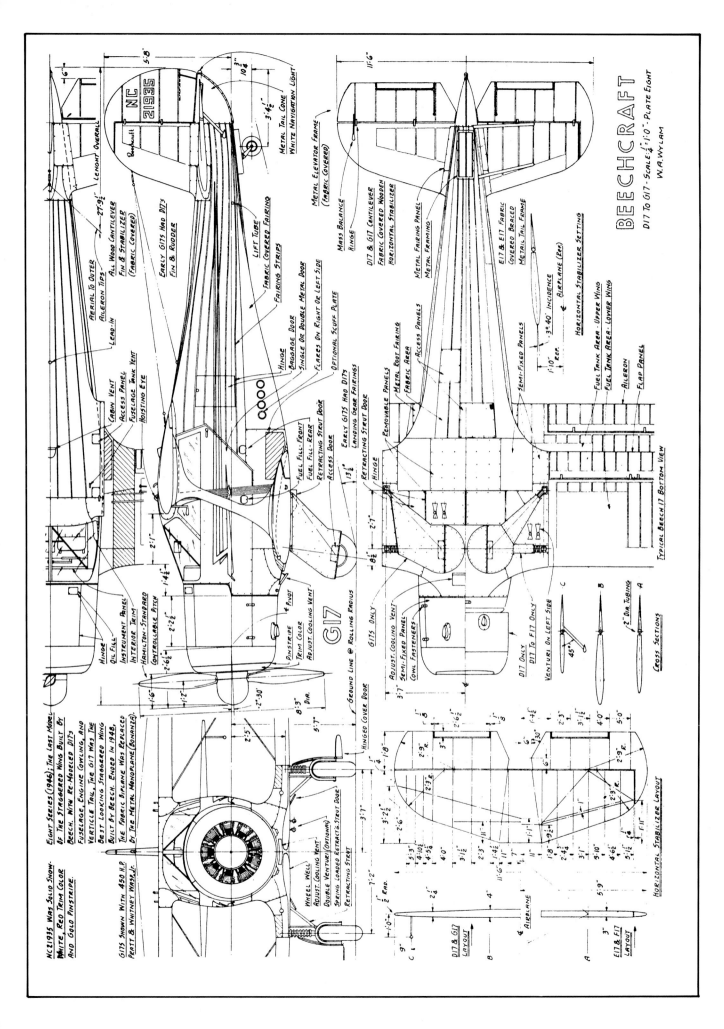

BEECHCRAFT
D17 To G17 · Scale ¼"=1'·0"· Plate Eight
W. A. Wylam

92

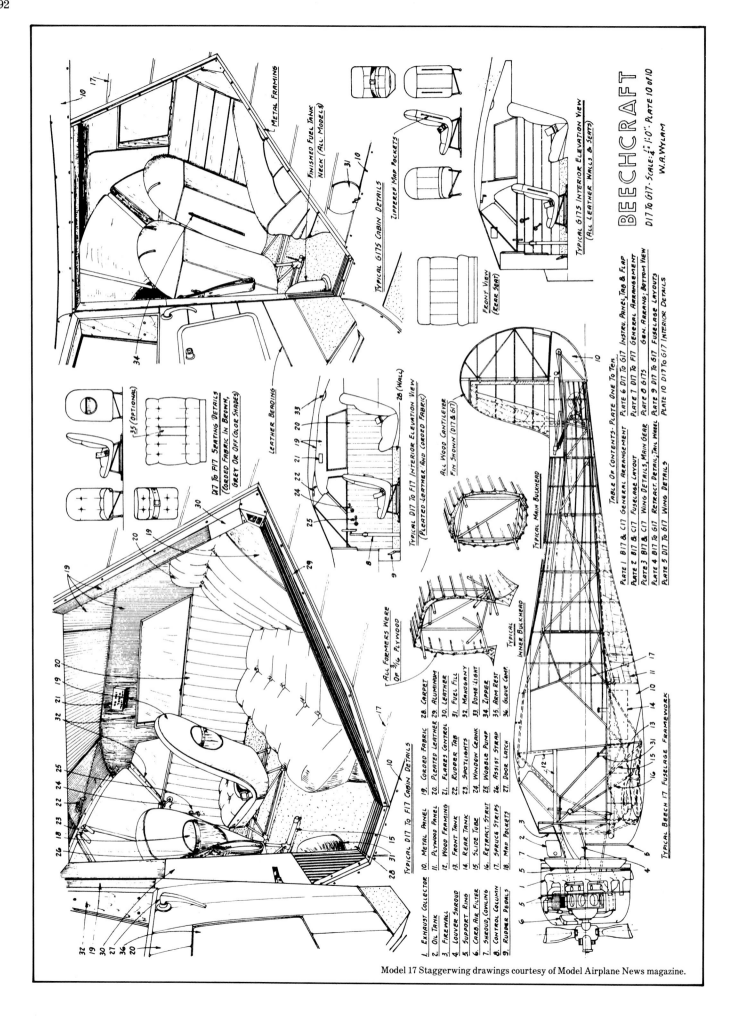

METAL FRAMING

FINISHED FUEL TANK
NECK (ALL MODELS)

ZIPPERED MAP POCKETS

TYPICAL 617S CABIN DETAILS

TYPICAL 617S INTERIOR ELEVATION VIEW
(ALL LEATHER WALLS & SEATS)

FRONT VIEW
(REAR SEAT)

BEECHCRAFT

D17 TO G17 · SCALE: ¼"=1'-0" · PLATE 10 of 10
W. A. WYLAM

35 (OPTIONAL)

D17 TO F17 SEATING DETAILS
(CORDED FABRIC IN BROWN,
GREY OR OFF COLOR SHADES)

LEATHER BENDING

28 (WALL)

TYPICAL D17 TO F17 INTERIOR ELEVATION VIEW
(PLEATED LEATHER AND CORDED FABRIC)

ALL WOOD CANTILEVER
FIN SHOWN (D17 & G17)

TYPICAL MAIN BULKHEAD

ALL FORMERS WERE
OF 3/16 PLYWOOD

TYPICAL
INNER BULKHEAD

TYPICAL D17 TO F17 CABIN DETAILS

10. METAL PANEL   19. CORDED FABRIC   28. CARPET
11. PLYWOOD PANEL   20. PLEATED LEATHER   29. ALUMINUM
12. WOOD FRAMING   21. FLARES CONTROL   30. LEATHER
13. FRONT TANK   22. RUDDER TAB   31. FUEL FILL
14. REAR TANK   23. SPOTLIGHTS   32. MAHOGANY
15. SLIDE TUBE   24. WINDOW CRANK   33. DOME LIGHT
16. RETRACT. STRUT   25. WOBBLE PUMP   34. ZIPPER
17. SPRUCE STRIPS   26. ASSIST STRAP   35. ARM REST
18. MAP POCKETS   27. DOOR LATCH   36. GLOVE COMP.

1. EXHAUST COLLECTOR
2. OIL TANK
3. FIREWALL
4. LOUVER SHROUD
5. SUPPORT RING
6. CARB. AIR FILTER
7. SHROUD, COWLING
8. CONTROL COLUMN
9. RUDDER PEDALS

TYPICAL BEECH 17 FUSELAGE FRAMEWORK

Model 17 Staggerwing drawings courtesy of Model Airplane News magazine.

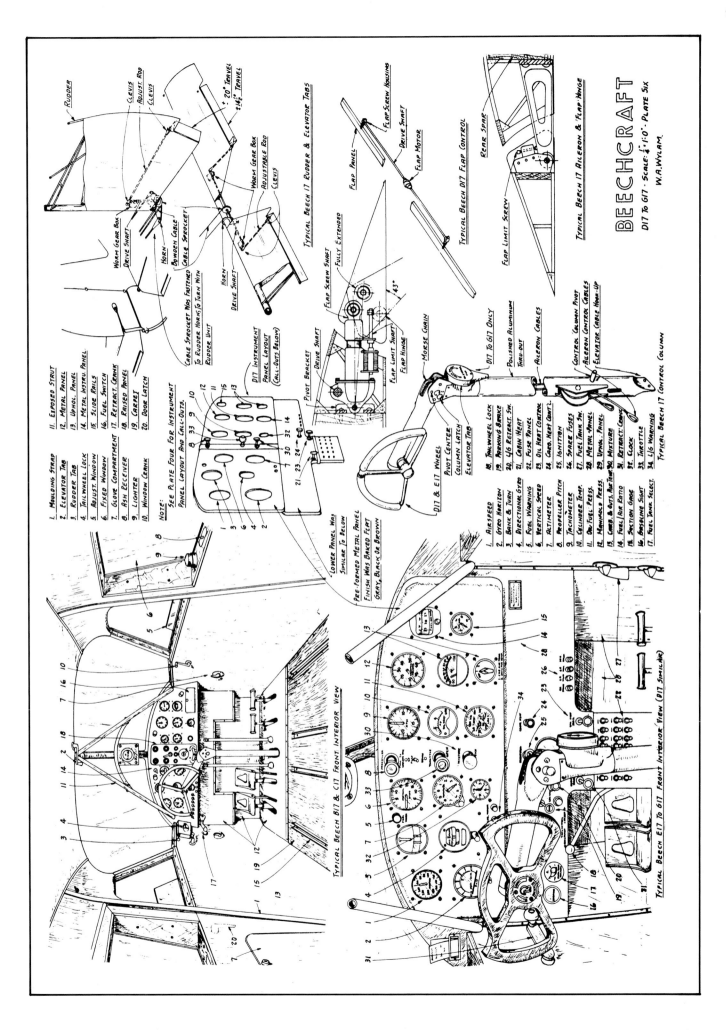

BEECHCRAFT

D17 TO G17 · SCALE ¼"·1'·0" · PLATE SIX

W.A.WYLAM.

Typical Beech 17 Aileron & Flap Hinge

Typical Beech D17 Flap Control

Typical Beech 17 Rudder & Elevator Tabs

Typical Beech 17 Control Column

Typical Beech B17 & C17 Front Interior View

Typical Beech E17 To G17 Front Interior View (D17 Similar)

1. MOULDING STRAP
2. ELEVATOR TAB
3. RUDDER TAB
4. TAILWHEEL LOCK
5. ADJUST. WINDOW
6. FIXED WINDOW
7. GLOVE COMPARTMENT
8. ASH RECEIVER
9. LIGHTER
10. WINDOW CRANK
11. EXPOSED STRUT
12. METAL PANEL
13. UPHOL. PANEL
14. METAL INSTRU PANEL
15. SLIDE RAILS
16. FUEL SWITCH
17. RETRACT. CRANK
18. RAISED PANEL
19. CARPET
20. DOOR LATCH

NOTE:
SEE PLATE FOUR FOR INSTRUMENT
PANEL LAYOUT AND CALL-OUTS.

D17 INSTRUMENT
PANEL LAYOUT
(CALL-OUTS BELOW)

LOWER PANEL WAS
SIMILAR TO BELOW

PRE-FORMED METAL PANEL
FINISH WAS BAKED FLAT
GRAY, BLACK OR BROWN

1. AIRSPEED
2. GYRO HORIZON
3. BANK & TURN
4. DIRECTIONAL GYRO
5. FUEL WARNING
6. VERTICAL SPEED
7. ALTIMETER
8. PROPELLER PITCH
9. TACHOMETER
10. CYLINDER TEMP.
11. MANIFOLD PRESS.
12. OIL FUEL PRESS.
13. CARB. & OUTS. AIR TEMP.
14. FUEL /AIR RATIO
15. SUCTION GAGE
16. GASOLINE SIGHT
17. FUEL TANK SELECT.
18. TAILWHEEL LOCK
19. PARKING BRAKE
20. L/G RETRACT. SW.
21. CABIN HEAT
22. FUSE PANEL
23. OIL HEAT CONTROL
24. CARB. HEAT CONTROL
25. IGNITION
26. SPARE FUSES
27. FUEL TANK. SW.
28. METAL PANEL
29. UPHOL. PANEL
30. MIXTURE
31. RETRACT. CRANK
32. CLOCK
33. THROTTLE
34. L/G WARNING

RUDDER
CLEVIS
ADJUST. ROD
CLEVIS
+ 20° TRAVEL
± 14½° TRAVEL
WORM GEAR BOX
DRIVE SHAFT
HORN
BOWDEN CABLE
CABLE SPROCKET
WORM GEAR BOX
ADJUSTABLE ROD
CLEVIS
HORN
DRIVE SHAFT
CABLE SPROCKET NO.S FASTENED
TO RUDDER HORN & TO TURN WITH
RUDDER UNIT

FLAP SCREW HOUSING
FLAP PANEL
DRIVE SHAFT
FLAP MOTOR
REAR SPAR
FLAP LIMIT SCREW
FLAP SCREW SHAFT
FULLY EXTENDED
43°
MOOSE CHAIN
FLAP LIMIT SHAFT
FLAP HINGE
PIVOT BRACKET
DRIVE SHAFT

D17 TO G17 ONLY
POLISHED ALUMINUM
THRU-OUT
AILERON CABLES
CONTROL COLUMN PIVOT
AILERON CONTROL CABLES
ELEVATOR CABLE HOOK-UP
D17 & E17 WHEEL
PIVOT CENTER
COLUMN LATCH
ELEVATOR TAB

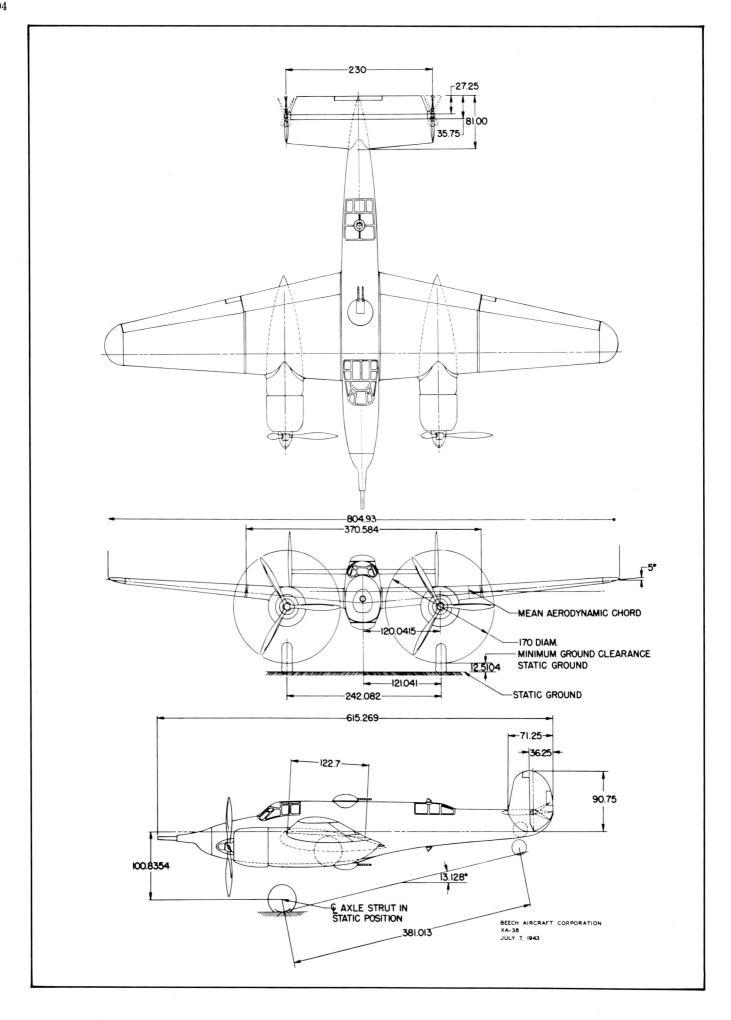

230

27.25

81.00

35.75

804.93

370.584

5°

MEAN AERODYNAMIC CHORD

170 DIAM.

MINIMUM GROUND CLEARANCE
STATIC GROUND

120.0415

12.5104

STATIC GROUND

121.041

242.082

615.269

71.25

36.25

122.7

90.75

100.8354

13.128°

€ AXLE STRUT IN
STATIC POSITION

381.013

BEECH AIRCRAFT CORPORATION
XA-38
JULY 7, 1943

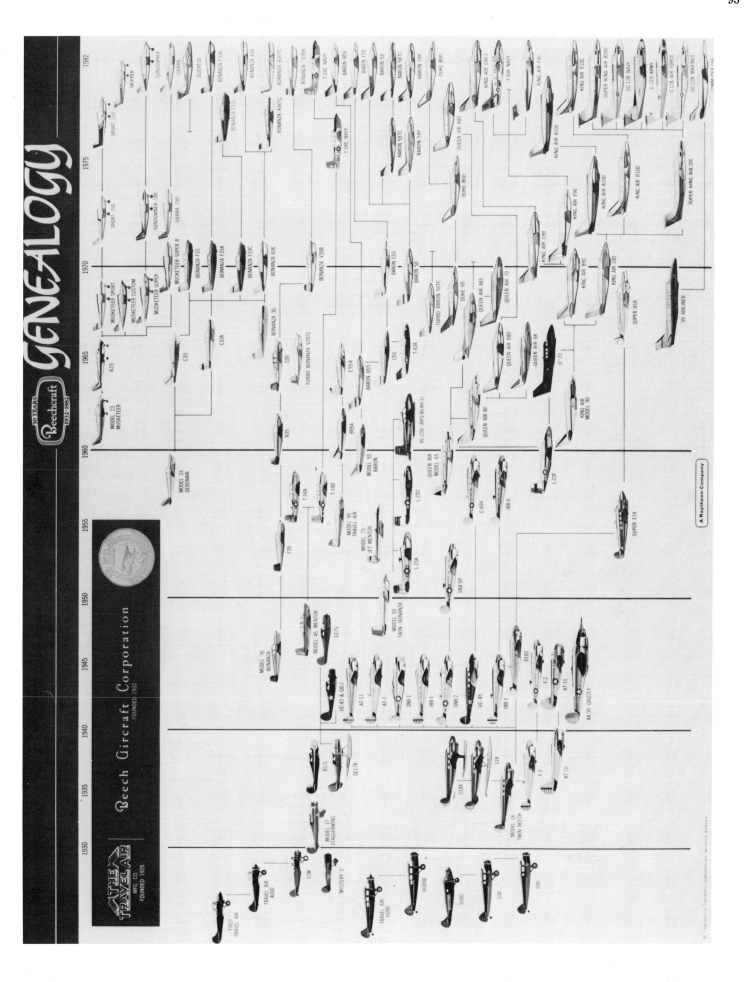

96

INDEX

Back cover: D18's on the line, 1946. Photo by Victor Keppler.